Aromatherapy

A Symphony of Colored Energy and Aromatic Scents

(Holistic Natural Healing Powers of Essential Oils for the Mind Body Spirit and Comfort Zones)

David Burman

Published By **Chris David**

David Burman

Aromatherapy: A Symphony of Colored Energy and Aromatic Scents (Holistic Natural Healing Powers of Essential Oils for the Mind Body Spirit and Comfort Zones)

ISBN 978-1-998038-35-0

No part of this guidebook shall be reproduced in any form without permission in writing from the publisher except in the case of brief quotations embodied in critical articles or reviews.

Legal & Disclaimer

Table Of Contents

Chapter 1: Aromatherapy

The Aromatherapy branch is part of Phytotherapy and is an integral an element of Non-Conventional Medicine (MNC). It makes use of the high-powered flying chemicals extracted from plants and transformed to essential oils.

The term Aromatherapy is a term used to describe something useful that can be absorbed by the senses. The Aromatherapy branch of the MNC uses the inhalation and absorption of components emanating directly from the essential oils.

The chemical compounds are that are naturally produced by oxygen amino acids and minerals obtained from natural resins flowers, seeds, leaves or barks. They also contain berries and.

Aromatherapy's purpose is to provide physical, emotional and spiritual well-being by a holistic method.

Inhaling the scents stimulates the limbic system in the brain and connects it to memories of emotional archaically.

It's used in particular an attempt to prevent and restore the overall wellbeing. Oils aid us to maintain our emotional and energetic equilibrium, and prevent the development of imbalances that can turn into actual ailments.

Aromatherapy is one of the non-traditional treatments and is one of the treatments that has a powerful connections to nature's energy forces. When you utilize essential oils within it, you are able to feel the power of elements, such as earth water, fire as well as the wind. The energy of these elements is transferred to us and give our physical, mental, and mental wellbeing.

HISTORY OF THE AROMATHERAPY

Since the dawn of time mankind has made use of every natural resource available at various locations, including plants, resins, and flowers in order to treat himself while performing holy rituals. The year was 5000 a.C In India In the sacred text of Brahma (from where comes the term Ayurveda) the authors have described the secret of longevity through the suggestion of using fragrant plants from the Middle East in 4000 a.C. At 2800 a.C within the time of the Chinese Empire the Chinese Empire disseminated the wisdom of herbs and the extracts they produced. In Egypt at the time of 2700 a.C people used essential oils for wellness beauty, rituals, and health. Aromatherapy was a common practice across cultures around all over the world.

The healers, also known as the shamans or wise utilized the oils to achieve various antibacterial benefits as well as analgesics and anti-inflammatory effects. along with rites and religious connection.

Then, in the subsequent decades, we've come to the distillation process of today that was developed in the Arabian alchemists around the X century a.C.

It was the Middle Age, near the date of 1,000 d.C. through alchemy and hermetical science, that was developed the first modern method of distillation, Avicenna's Alembic.

Then, in the subsequent periods and the following periods, the Spagyric Art and the Quintessence emerged.

ANATOMY AND CHEMICALS OF THE PLANTS

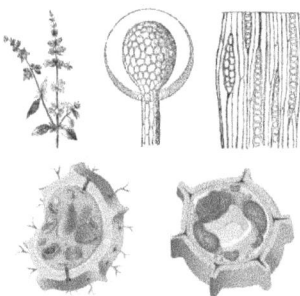

The anatomy of plants serves as the foundation to understand how essential oils are beneficial that work in conjunction with the human body.

Within the cell took place chemical synthesizing processes, referred to as "metabolites", which are essential for growth as well as the life of the plant.

By photosynthesis, plants integrate carbon atoms and oxygen and hydrogen atoms. They are then bonded with minerals found in the air, earth, water as well as the surrounding environment provide the basis for secondary metabolites which are beneficial for our health. Organic chemistry is founded on carbon and the majority of the oils are made up of unsaturated hydrocarbons referred to as "terpenes". They are made from the mevalonate acids or activated Acetyl.

EXTRACTION TECHNIQUES

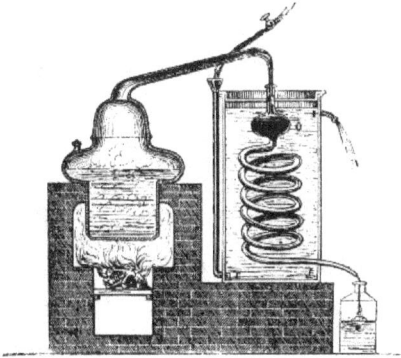

Extraction methods for essential oils include a variety of.

The most popular ones include:

The steam-driven distillation process;

The Pressing;

The Enfleurage

The extraction process is done using alcohol derived from vegetable sources.

The extraction process is carried out using solvents.

In this article, we'll examine the most popular methods, such as the distillation using steam flow as well as pressing.

The process of distillation using steam flow can be used in plants that have not been affected due to the heat. The plant material is placed into a tub in which the steam that is pressured flows through the substance and oils move via the steam. As the steam cools and the essences pass through a tube which separates them into two parts that are essential oils as well as the water for flowers.

The temperature as well as the press are the two most important factors that make a premium essential oil.

The process of pressing is utilized for the citrus fruits since their juice must be crushed to get the oils that are contained.

THE OLFACTORY SYSTEM

From an anatomical as well as a functional perspective from an anatomical and functional point of view, the human olfactory organ is incredibly complex and fascinating (just consider how your brain is able to store the scents of over a thousand). In this book, I'd like readers to comprehend the way the sense of smell is connected with your daily life in order to get all the benefits.

The olfactory system is the nose, through which we come in contact with the air and scent particles. The particles dissolve within the production of a chemical and then bond with the millions of receivers placed onto the olfactive cell's eyelashes. It is a specialized chemical sense and the olfactive cells constitute the sole place within the human body that the nervous system of central nerves can be directly in contact with the outside world. The scent's molecules travel through the olfactive nerve, where there are neurons which control emotions and memory. They then reach the central nerve of the brain, which generates the answer. Signals from organs that sense, first they get to the thalamus. After that, through an electrical circuit formed by a strand of nerve fibers, coming out of the thalamus, they land in the amygdala. It is the area that sends messages into the hypothalamus. The stimulation of the sympathetic nervous system is believed to be at the heart for the integration of superior neurologic functions like emotion. There is no doubt that the amygdala can be implicated in emotional memory system and in processing the stimulus acquired through previous memories and also the olfactive system. This is the reason why emotions connected to smells and which are the basis of learning and, in particular the way that a baby can detect the mother's scent, particularly via the sense of smell. This may seem unbelievable however, an oil reaches the brain in just 22 seconds, and the flow of blood within 2 minutes, and the cells in just the body takes 20 minutes.

In order to make the olfactory system and its function understandable It is helpful to consider it to be brain software. When it is in contact with certain scents, it transmits signals to the parasympathetic and sympathetic nerve system, triggering hormone production which triggers within us an physical, emotional and energetic response. The scents' notes interact with oil essentials.

FRAGRANCES' NOTES

He notes in the scents of essential oils represent an element of "volatility", that is the period during which essential oils begin to evaporate when they are exposed to the air.

The notes are subdivided into:

From the top or high;

From the middle, or in the heart;

From base or low;

The high notes, or the sound of your head, is the first sensation you experience disappear in short duration. They are the result of juices and fruits. They can be stimulating and energizing and include:

Lemon;

Tangerine;

Orange;

Bergamot.

The middle notes, or those that come from the heart, tend to will last for a while and have a more sensual tone or enveloping, and also flowering. These originate from stems or petals for example:

Ylang-ylang;

Cloves;

Fennel;

Lavender;

Geranium;

Chamomile;

Jasmine.

The notes below are made up of essential oils that will last for a long time and make up the essence of a perfume, such as the spicy and woody scent that includes:

Cedarwood;

Incense;

Myrrh;

Vetiver;

Patchouli;

Sandal;

Also, there are families of perfumes which belong to essential oils.

Citrus:

In addition to oils like the Wilde citrus, lemon, lime, and bergamot. Citruses scents tend to be refreshing and stimulating that have a refreshing and fresh aroma with a bitter note. These notes of citruses are usually those of the mind. They're photosensitive, so shouldn't be utilized prior to exposure to sunlight or UV Rays.

Spiced:

The spices possess a pleasant scent while some balsamic varieties are antibacterial. The oils are warm, and they need to be reduced further. This includes cinnamon, black pepper, and cassia.

Herbals:

They are clear and have a clean scent. Many are part of middle notes. They include rosemary, thyme and patchouli.

Woody:

Woody scents range between the middle and center. The scents they emit are roots and stabilizing like the tree's roots of which they are derived. A lot of them have an intense scent as well as a woody, enveloping scent similar to fruity wood, sandal and arborvitae.

Floral:

Flower oils comprise the majority of middle notes. They tend to be sweet and fragranced They are also very similar to the flowers they are from, such as lavender Geranium, and ylang ylang.

Minty:

Perfusive and refreshing scents like as peppermint and green mint.

Earth:

The oils have an almost smoky fragrance that is similar to earth like the violet.

Chapter 2: Using Of The Essential Oils

Essential oils are utilized to:

Topic;

Aromatic;

Intern;

This chapter we're going to examine the aromatic and topical usage, as the essential oil must be handled with care as well as under the guidance of a medical professional for essential pure as well as certificate oils.

Aromatic use

The best method to reap the benefits of essential oils at an aroma level is through the use of the cold diffuser as it lets the particles breathe out smelling with the correct way, and without modifying the scent. By allowing the diffusion to be cold that occurs, the smell detector instantly absorbs the oil, and then it triggers a swift reaction to the limbic system that is linked to the memory of emotions. If there isn't an diffuser, then a couple of drops could be placed into the palm of one's hand. Then it is necessary to rub them and then breathed in. Diffused oils increase oxygen levels, create negative ions and create naturally ozone, contrasting unpleasant smells, and cleansing the air. A variety of essential oils, such as citrus, lemongrass, grapefruit, eucalyptus and thyme, as well as lavender, citrus, and incense have a great ability to ward off the batters and germs that are present within the air. Additionally, some drops of oils could be put into an unbleached napkin, and be smelt whenever one would like to.

Topic use

The method of topical application is suggested and employed when using MTC treatments because it permits to reach every cell, giving the beneficial components of the aroma. It is essential to choose pure oils since our skin levels absorb all the elements (I utilize edible ones for the assurance of the high quality). Essential oils can have numerous beneficial benefits that extend beyond your body. Certain oils possess relaxing, soothing, and grounding qualities, whereas other oils are stimulating, revitalizing or rejuvenating.

It's not advised to use the oil in its pure form directly on your skin however, they must be dilute with a variety of vectorial oils so that you reap the most advantages and to avoid any irritation. There are warm oils characteristics that need to be dilute by 10%, which are the ones which are produced by animals because they cause irritation and are warm when used in pure form or undiluted. A different method to prevent issues related to photosensitivity is not using citrus oils before we expose ourselves to sun.

Essential oils are applied directly to the skin or scalp. It is a great idea to massage the scalp in diverse Chinese medical practices and for working on the lines of meridian.

Carrier oils

The oils of Vector must be vegetable that are derived from fruits or seeds that are press cold. It is better to use bio-based. For them to be able to move more efficiently, it's important to select the correct diluting method.

Fractioned coconut oil is rich in antioxidants as well as vitamin E. Coconut oil that is virgin cannot be absorbed as quickly by the skin. Therefore, it is advised to choose using the fractioned oil. The fat acids are separated in order to create a non-grease based oil that is lightweight and good to observe the oil.

Sweet almond oil can be beneficial for all skin types as well as applications for topical use. It's absorbed easily by the skin and is pleasant to the nose as well as being good to use for facial skincare.

Jojoba oil oil is a liquid. It's a gold-colored oil which doesn't have any smell. Jojoba is a well-known vector oil since it's good for hair and helps to keep the skin moist. It's akin to the oil that is naturally produced by our skin, and can be utilized for a grease skin kind.

Grape seed oil contains a significant amount of Linoleic acid, which is very hydrating and beneficial for people with people with sensitive skin. It has a light and sweet smell, it's an excellent oil for vectors for use when you have age spots.

Argan oil: It is very nourishing, with an aroma reminiscent of nuts. It is rich in vitamin A as well as E as well as monosaturated fat acids beneficial for hair and body.

Avocado oil: It is a rich oil in the oleic acid (a monounsaturated fat acid) beneficial for dry and damaged skin. It's nourishing as well as a good suggestion for skin that is aging.

Chapter 3: Chinese Medicine

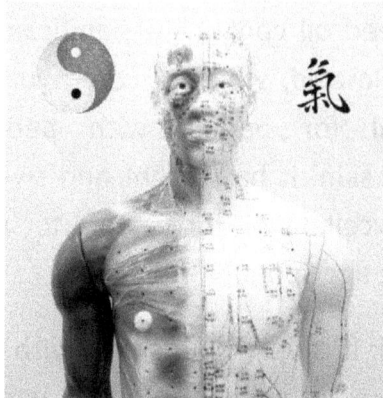

The energetic energy that is associated with Chinese medical and philosophy known as MTC It is the energy that is thin, referred to as vital lymph, or breath of vitality. In the MTC it is known as Ki or QI in Japanese.

The Qi notion at the heart of all the philosophy, culture and Chinese Medicine is the energy which gives life to all things.

It is everywhere and circulated throughout our body, as well as in the limbs of thin people by circulating through the energetic channels of the meridian.

The concept of energy is that, by moving through the channels, also known as Meridian It maintains the equilibrium and well-being. When there's a disturbance or an energy blockage that is not able to circulate through the channels, and it manifests as discomfort.

According to Chinese Medicine the organism is considered to be a microcosm within the microcosms. It is an element of the whole which is extremely complex and controlled by the energy and determination actions by interconnected fundamentals. The roles of the entire body are controlled by:

The basic principle behind Yin organs is that they are full and the Yang empty Entrails.

Meridians;

The five elements of

Three essential jewels:

The process that goes into the entire process.

In Chinese medicine, there exist two main energies that contribute to the balance of energy: Yin and Yang.

YIN AND YANG ENERGIES

This Yin energy is feminine, soft, humid, and sensitive, and linked with the moon and the night, and to winter. The meridians that are linked to it comprise six and originate through the organs.

The Yang male is hot, dry, tough and active. It is linked with the sun and the sun and to the summer. The meridians that are linked to it originate from the digestive tract. They are both complementary as well as indistinguishable elements. They are both essential and the balance between them remains constant and fluctuating. A balance of both is what makes healthy physical, mental and energy health. There is no imbalance or disease that is made up of yin and Yang and both are interconnected to one another even during the phases of discord.

MERIDIANS

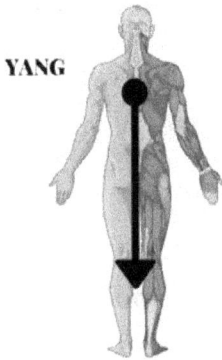

YANG

Within the body, there 14 meridians in the body each of which is linked to an organ. The Yang meridians are found in the posterior

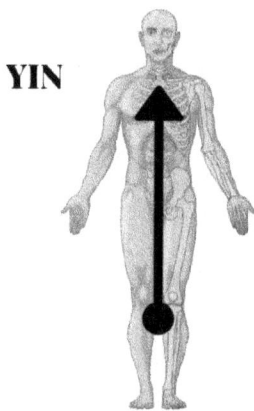

YIN

region of the body, where energies flow low.

The Yang meridians lie located in the front of the body, where energy flows towards the higher.

Each meridian is connected and the next one follows at a particular point, allowing for the Qi energy to flow forward.

The process is carried out through a repeating cycle that sees energy circulates throughout all of the body. The Governor Vassel Meridian is located posteriorly, while it is the Conception Vassel is the one in front, and are considered exceptional in that, unlike the other meridians and always in motion.

The Meridians:

Lung meridian;

Big intestine meridian;

Stomach meridian;

Spleen meridian;

The Heart Meridian;

Small Intestine Meridian

Bladder meridian

Kidney Meridian;

Heart minister meridian;

Triple warmer Meridian (linked with the heart).

Gall bladder Meridian (linked with gallbladder).

Meridian of the Liver;

Gov vessel;

Conception vessel

The Body Meridians

According to MTC that the manifesting of a symptom and its manifestation in the body, as well as at an energy and emotional level results from pain or restriction of energy along meridians.

The energy flow is at the heart of all therapies, including:

Reflexology;

Kinesiology;

Acupuncture;

Tuina;

Shiatsu;

Qi Gong;

and other therapies in the MTC.

The Meridians are connected by a unique and powerful circuit which extends the 24-hour circadian cycle:

From 03:00 to 5:00 Lung.

From 05:00 to 7:00 Large Intestine.

From 07:00 to 9:00 Stomach.

From 09:00 to 11:00 Spleen.

From 11:00 to 13:00 Hearth.

From 13:00 to 15:00 Small Intestine.

From 15:00 to 17:00 Bladder.

From 17:00 to 19:00 Kidney.

Chapter 4: The Elements

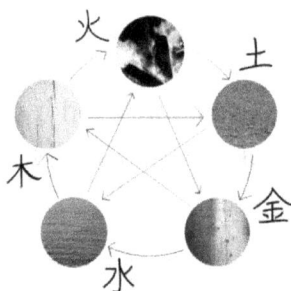

Beyond the circle of circadian rhythms, Chinese traditional medicine, the system of healing is built on the five elements that make up nature:

Water;

Wood;

Fire;

Earth;

Metal;

Water

The water's connection is to winter. It also connects with the Yin in the kidney as well as it is connected to the Yang in the bladder.

It's the one responsible for the power of will. It also displays wisdom. The emotional states associated with this element include love and fear, as well as stress. The harmony that is associated with the element of water can make us more focused, wise and innovative. Discord makes us feel numb anxious, uneasy, and nervous.

Rebalancing essential oils are:

Cedarwood;

Geranium;

Ginger;

Juniper Berry;

Thymes;

Wood

Wood elements that are connected to the spring. It is connected with the Yin that is the liver as well as it is linked to the Yang in the gallbladder. It's the manifestation of the soul's ethereal nature and displays empathy. The emotions associated with this element is generosity, anger, jealousy or even discontent. Harmony of the wood element is able to keep us more organized and focused. Unbalance can cause us to be anxious, rigid, aggressive or angry.

Essential oils for rebalancing

Bergamot;

chamomile;

grapefruit;

Sweet orange

Fire

The element of fire is connected with the season, the heart's yin and to the Yang that is in our small intestinal tract. It helps to regulate our minds and is a manifestation of the love.

The feelings of fire include emotions of love, joy, or insecurity. When the elements of fire are harmonious, we are calm, happy and wise and sane. Otherwise, we feel agitated, anxious, hypersensitive and uncomfortable.

It's linked to the energy force that creates wealth.

Essential oils to rebalance:

jasmine;

bay;

lavender;

lemon balm;

neroli;

palmarose;

rose;

rosemary;

Spikenard,

ylang ylang.

Earth

The earth element is tied to the conclusion of season, it being the Yin in the spleen, and to the Yang that is in our stomachs. It rewires our brain and is an expression of empathy.

The emotions that make up the Earth are fairness, open-mindedness as well as anxiety, worry and preoccupation. If it's in balance, it allows us to be helpful compassionate, cautious and kind, in contrast, it leaves us uncertain, overprotective, and unclear. It's connected to the stability energy.

Essential oils to rebalance:

benzoin;

cardamom;

frankincense;

lemon;

marjoram,

myrrh;

patchouli;

peppermint;

sandalwood;

vetiver.

Metal

Metal elements are connected to the fall, the lungs of the Yin and Yang, as well as the large stomach. This is how our body's soul gets adjusted as well as being the symbol of respect.

Metal's emotional facets include bravery, courage and depression.

Chapter 5: Emotions And Organs

To use Chinese medical treatment, the organs of our body also contain emotions. There was a certain emotion, and you felt as though it was a specific discomfort in one particular region within your body.

Then there's a diagram of the emotional states as well as the organs that are related:

Angry - Liver

Joy- Heart

The sadness and pain of the Lungs

Concern - Spleen

Fear - Kidneys

Scare, Shock- Gallbladder

Essential oils and aromatherapy may assist us in balancing of emotional states by through the application of the fundamentals of the energy systems that are part of Chinese medicine.

ACUPUNCTURE

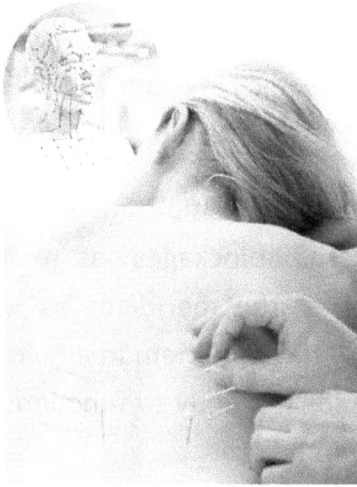

Acupuncture is one of the branches that is part of Traditional Chinese medicine that was developed hundreds decades ago. It was accepted in the OMS and is now widely used throughout the West. Nowadays, it is utilized in a myriad of fields of medicine for treating physical (articulatory headaches and pains) as well as emotional (stress anxious, panic or anxiety attacks) disorders. In order to get the treatment you need it is recommended to seek out experts in this area.

The word is taken from the Latin word "acus" (needle) and punctural (puncture). It is the process of puncturing the skin with a certain number of needles in order in order to trigger the vital points in the meridians of our bodies.

Acupuncture is a method of working to eliminate the blockages as well as the imbalances of the meridians as when Qi is able to flow through them in a fluid manner it is possible for the body to function and is in a good state of health.

MOXIBUSTION AND CUPPING

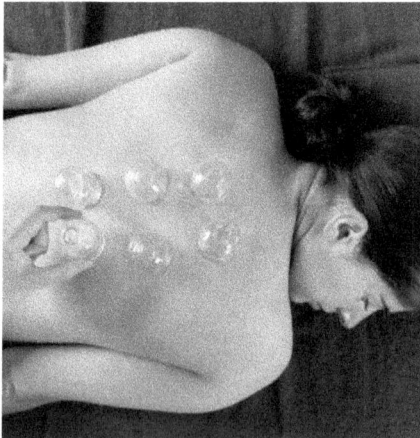

In addition to acupuncture, there are other methods that are more gentle and work on the same basis as the acupunctures. They work by stimulating the meridians channel in order to balance the Qi.

The Moxibustion utilizes warm temperatures to stimulate points by using warm needles.

Cupping utilizes glass cups to improve the Qi circulation in certain areas of the body. They are the most effective method to alleviate muscular pain and spasms. It also helps in clearing the body of toxins.

ACUPRESSURE

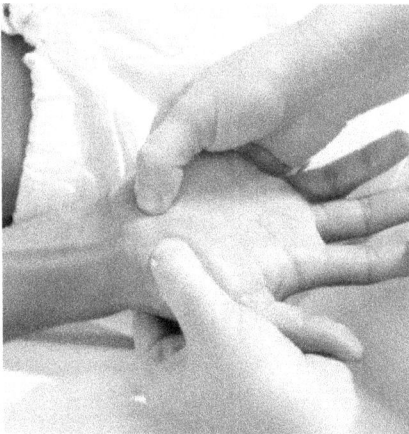

Acupressure is an non-invasive procedure, as it does not require needles, instead it makes finger and hand movements.

The meridians' acupuncture points are stimulated with a hand in order to balance the energies of Qi.

Essential oils as well as aromatherapy is well-integrated into this method (we will look into the specifics of the essential oils and their properties).

TUI NA

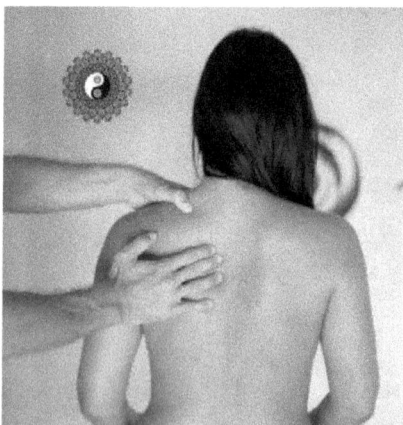

He Tui Na is considered to be one of the top manipulative treatments whose origins lie from the Shand Dynasty.

Its primary goal of use is to identify tight and stiff zones or points that are painful, and by focusing on them, you can let the energy flow in a correct manner. This practice is accompanied by with oils and herbs that add to the Mio relaxation process more comfortable. The practice is widespread across the western world as well as in conjunction in martial arts it's useful to maintain the Qi flowing in a balanced manner.

TAI CHI

Tai-Chi is a traditional Chinese martial art that is based upon the Taoist idea of Yin-Yang. Tai Chi Chuan means "supreme fighting art". Through the ages when it was refined, it was a popular training method that was able to boost prosperity and well-being.

It's the result of a sequence of circular and slow movements that evoke the dance. The practice is beneficial for both body and mind. It serves to help the practitioner become aware of its own power as well as to better understand and to balance it.

Similar to similar to Qi notions of energy which circulate through the meridians Tai Chi, like acupuncture is a technique that works by removing the obstruction to flow, and brings harmony to the body.

QI GONG

It is the Qi Gong is an ancient martial art from the Taoist tradition. Literally, it is "to work with the energy".

It is where the energy is harnessed through the movement, breathing, and the meditation practices. The body is opened up to allow the Qi flows freely.

Chapter 6: Essential Oils In The Rebalance Of The Meridians

Essential oils as well as aromatherapy are effective instruments of assistance to utilize together with the energetic fundamentals of Traditional Chinese Medicine. The primary reason for the use of essential oils is provided in both the aromachemical chemicals of the plants as well as the power of those essential oils.

The essential oils are categorized as Yin or Yang in accordance with their speed of evaporation. Actually, the essential oil's classification is based on its time to evaporate. So, it's either forward, middle or the base note.

The characteristics that are energetic of Yin and Yang tell us how oils work.

Yang: It cools it helps relax, help to sleep, and it blocks, and absorbs, stores, produces and is moistening.

Yang is a warm and energized energy that can and energizes, triggers transformation, transfers, erases and shields.

ESSENTIAL OILS FOR YIN YANG TO REBALANCE THE MERIDIANS ACCORDING TO THE ELEMENTS

The Yin and Yang energy is constantly in shift and growth Sometimes, energy can become imbalanced in the body. The MTC is seeking to address the imbalance to ensure that we are body's the material and energy to a balanced way.

Wood: To this element is connected the Yang's lover and Yin's gall bladder, or. It is springtime and the perfect time to restore balance in the channel, and is known as "the palace of the wind". The meridians in the liver connect to tendons, muscles eyelashes, and nails. When these meridians are in discord are able to manifest emotions like anger. When it is at a level our bodies have a powerful determination-making abilities.

His energy is the main reason for the circulation and the regulation of Qi throughout the body. So, whenever there's less of it or the Qi is not strong enough it decreases the vitality and the overall health decreases.

For the benefit of essential oils, use the one that has been diluted along to the points of the meridian. Make use of the following:

Geranium

Bergamot;

Ginger;

Sage;

Lavender;

Lemon balm;

Neroli;

Ylang Ylang;

Orange;

Sandalwood;

Chamomile;

juniper berry;

Lemongrass;

Basil;

Marjoram;

Fennel;

Cardamom;

Mix them in accordance to wood elements

2 tablespoons carrier oil.

5 drops of essential lemongrass oil.

Four drops of essential ginger oil (reduce the dosage for people with those with sensitive skin).

Massage the mix to release the Yin and Yang of the Liver meridians, and the Yang of the Gall Bladder.

The element of fire are to this element are the Yin from the Heart meridians, as well as the Yang of the meridians in the small intestine. They are the triple warmers to the Yang as well as the pericardium to support the Yin. Within the heart is the Shen's headquarters. Shen that is connected to red, warm summer and bitterness. If the balance is maintained, it creates feelings of bliss in the form of joy, excitement as well as coping with anxiety. The meridian in the heart controls the heartbeat and circulation of blood throughout the body. When there is a discord, it exhibits changes to the cardiac rhythm like an anxiety and thirst, bitter taste in the mouth as well as short breath and heart palpitations.

The meridian that runs through the small intestine is accountable in supplying blood and nourishment and also for being emotionally tied to our will. When the meridian is affected it can cause a lot of the flow of urine, meteorism, or abdominal discomforts.

To reap the benefits of these oils, put them into vector oils, in areas where the meridian is. Make use of the following:

Rose;

Jasmine;

Ylang Ylang;

Neroli;

Sandalwood;

Frankincense;

Peppermint;

Cardamom;

2 tablespoons carrier oil;

5 drops rose essential oil.

Five drops Ylang Ylang essential oil.

Earth It is connected to Yin in the spleen, and it is also the Yang in the stomach. Its color is yellow. The taste is sweet and the time of year is ending in the summer. The muscles are controlled by the mouth.

If it's in balance, the state of emotional balance is compassion and cure for the other. When the opposite is true, and it causes anxiety. The meridians in the spleen connect to the creation of blood as well as the white globules are connected to the immune system. It is also involved in the mental process.

When the earth of meridians is in disarray, they may manifest as digestive issues as well as stress, lazyness, and anxiety. To reap the benefits of these oils, they should be reduced within the corresponding vector and place where meridians are. They are:

Rosemary

Thyme

Cardamom

Marjoram

Grapefruit

Lemon

Melissa

Hyssop

Basil

2 Tablespoons of carrier oils

5 drops of essential lemon oil

Five drops of essential fennel oil

Metal: The metal is associated with it being a part of the Yin in the lung, and The Yang of the large intestine in charge of the organs and the related processes.

Its color is white and the flavor is spicy and the time of year is autumn. Meridians can be emotionally represented through pain and sadness, and if they're not at a level, they could manifest as depression, an underlying feeling of heavyness, breathing difficulties and constipation or diarrhea. For the benefits of oils, they have to be mixed with the specific vector and placed where the meridians are. They are:

Chapter 7: Emotionally

Rose;

Bergamot;

Basil;

Geranium;

Ylang Ylang;

for bronchial congestions and constriction.

Eucalyptus;

Melaleuca;

Peppermint;

Sandalwood;

Rosemary;

Constipation can be caused by constipation.

Basil;

Fennel;

Marjoram;

Cumin;

Chamomile;

Rose;

For diarrhea:

Black pepper

Cloves;

Cypress;

Myrrh;

Mixture to treat bronchial congestion

2 tablespoons carrier oil

Three drops of peppermint.

Three drops of Eucalyptus.

Water: This element is associated the Yin in the kidney as well as the yang of the bladder. These control the filtering of organ's metabolites following the expulsion from the urine, and also the rest of the fluids. They are emotionally connected to courage and force in addition to sexuality. It is black in color. the flavor is salty, and the season is winter.

To reap the benefits of the oil, the oils must be dissolve in the vectors and place it where the meridians are. They are:

Juniper berry;

Cinnamon;

Ginger;

Melaleuca;

Rosemary;

Basil;

Cardamom;

Lemon grass

Jasmine;

Chamomile;

Patchouli;

Ylang Ylang;

Cedarwood;

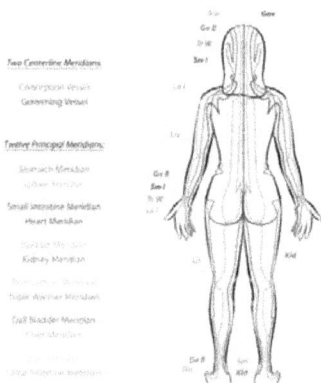

2 tablespoons carrier oil.

5 drops essential oil of jasmine.

Ten drops of chamomile essential oil.

ESSENTIAL OILS IN THE TRADITIONAL CHINESE MEDICINE

Cedarwood essential oil

The essential oil of cedarwood is used in Chinese medical practice, is an oil that has stabilizing characteristics, woody and sweet that helps balance the Shen and reduces the amount of humidity that is beneficial to the Yin. Additionally, it helps balance the kidneys' QI of energy and the organs associated with it. It also helps to balance breathing issues that can be attributed to mucus.

It's also beneficial when it's used as a an oil vector or a neutral cream to keep your hair and the skin shining. At the level of emotion it aids us in dealing with insomnia and anxiety through strengthening our will.

Topic Us: Put 12 drops of the oil in one teaspoon of the cream, or carrier oil.

Use for aromatherapy: Spread 4/5 drops of the oil in the diffuser.

Rosemary essential oil

The essential oil of rosemary found in Chinese treatment is a warming oil. properties. It promotes sweating, lowers humidity, and is an invigorator of the nervous system sympathetic. At a psychological level the oil promotes self-confidence and assists us in moving ahead. It's an effective solution to keep hair shiny and healthy. By using the topic method the oil is utilized as to warm your body, which can help alleviate discomforts and stimulating the mind.

Topical use 1 or 2 drops in shampoo, 2 drops of one teaspoon of oil vector for massaging an area of the body.

Use for aromatherapy: Add to the water in diffuser, 3-4 drops.

Basil essential oil

Basil essential oil found in Chinese remedies helps to strengthen the Yang energy in the kidney.

It also stimulates the nervous system. Therefore, it helps to combat fatigue and stress. In terms of emotional it helps to overcome the lack of faith.

The lumbar area is energized, which relieves your feeling of being heavy.

Topic usage: Add 3 drops to a teaspoon of oil for vector.

Use for aromatherapy: Add 3-4 drops to the diffuser.

Lavender essential oil

The lavender essential oil used in Chinese treatment is an oil that is associated with the lungs, the liver, as well as the pericardium. It assists in relaxing the mind, and it increases the Qi of the livers. it helps in the diffusion of breath Qi and release the warm wind.

It's great for nervousness as well as insomnia, irritability tension, and restlessness. It aids in the circulation of liver Qi (headaches spasms dysmenorrhea, hypertension) and also helps to calm the Shen (agitation anger, discontent, sleepiness). Additionally, it helps to spread the lungs' Qi (thoracic constriction as well as excessive breathing). It reduces the irritations to the skin and helps to nourish the skin.

Topical use: put 2/3 drops of the oil to 1 teaspoon of oil for vector.

Use for aromatherapy: Add 3-4 drops of essential oil into the diffuser.

Chapter 8: Frankincense Essential Oil

The essential oil of incense in Chinese treatment is believed to balance the liver, spleen, as well as the meridians in the heart. The incense oil has always been utilized in spiritual rituals in all societies It is beneficial to focus and meditate on the spiritual aspect. It helps to improve mental clarity and focus, in addition helping to heal emotional and physical wounds. It can be used to regenerate cells.

Topical use: Add 2/3 drops to one tablespoon of carrier oil.

For aromatic purposes, add 3 or 4 drops of the oil into the diffuser.

Lemon essential oil

The essential oil of lemon is used in Chinese remedies has cool, refreshing and tonic vitality. It assists in the connection between your heart as well as mind. Additionally, it's an effective antiseptic. It clears the Qi in the gallbladder and helps move the remaining Qi to aid digestion.

In terms of emotional energy, it brings joy and happiness.

Topical use: put 2/3 drops to 1 spoon of oil for vector.

Use for aromatherapy: Add 3-4 drops into the diffuser.

N.B It is sensitive to light, so avoid usage when in the sun or exposed to UV radiations.

Ylang Ylang essential oil

There is Ylang Ylang essential oil used in Chinese medicine is a gorgeous essential oil, extracted by the steam of flowers. It works well to the Heart's meridian. It helps to balance Shen's issues as well as the lack of kidney's essential. It is aphrodisiac in nature. In terms of emotional benefits, it's a great note for bringing calm and equilibrium on the physical and mental as well as emotional as well as a spiritual dimension. When used in a way that is topical, it will nourish your the skin and hair.

Topic usage: Add 2-3 drops of the oil in one teaspoon of the vector oil in addition to the shampoo amount.

For aromatic purposes, add 3 - 4 drops into the diffuser.

Essential oils derived from Seeds

Three examples of common essential oils that are derived directly from plant seeds are

1.Cardamom (Ellettaria cardamomum)--the most essential of oils comes from the family Zingiberaceae. The uses of this oil are antifungal, antibacterial as well as an antispasmodic, aphrodisiac and expectorant, digestive stimulant stimulation of the parasympathetic nervous system as well as stimulant and tonic.

2.Black pepper (Piper Nigra) comes from the family Piperaceae. The uses for this oil are the use of an analgesic and antiseptic; the antispasmodic, antitoxic digestion, circulatory, and digestive tonic. It can reduce pain and fever and a rubefacient as well as for stimulating.

3.Sweet Fennel (Foeniculum vulgare, var. dulce) comes from the family called Apiaceae. It is as an antibacterial, anti-inflammatory and antifungal agent, as well as an antispasmodic digestion aid, as well as in relieving gas.

Essential oils from stems Leaf, Needles, and Stems

Seven common instances of essential oils that are derived from leaves, stems and even needles.

1.Cistus (Cistus ladanifer) comes from the family Cistaceae. Essential oil derived from twigs, stems, dried leaves, as well as dried flowers. It is used as a cicatrizant, or for rejuvenation of cells, for its antibacterial and anti-infectious properties antimicrobial, an astringent, as well as antiviral substance; as an immune booster and regulator, as a tonic and a support to the central and parasympathetic nervous system; as well as for wound healing.

2.Eucalyptus is a species of tree belonging to the family of plants Myrtaceae. It is also known with many different terms, including eucalyptus oil oil blue mallee, and the gully gum oil. Leaves and twigs can be employed to treat wounds, burns and nasal congestion. They also help in reducing nasal congestion, blood glucose as well as asthma, and also for an insect repellent. Also, it is utilized in supplements and medications.

3.Laurel (Laurus nobilis) is a member of the family of plants known as Lauraceae. This evergreen, aromatic scrub is well-known for its aromatic dark green glossy leaves. Fresh and dried leaves oil can be used to treat analgesia and antibacterial. It is also an antimicrobial an antispasmodic, antiseptic and antiviral. They are used for increasing the immune system, and for calm the nervous system in addition, it is used as an expectorant as well as an insecticide.

4.Patchouli (Pogostemon cablin) originates from the family Lamiaceae which is also known as the dead needle or mint active plant. The oil extracted from the leaves is used for antidepressants, anti-inflammatory as well as antiviral, antimicrobial an aphrodisiac and astringent. It is also used as and digestion aid; alleviating gas and relaxing the nervous system as well as for stimulant and tonic.

5.Peppermint (Mentha Piperita x) is a member of the family of plants Lamiacae within the mint family. Essential oil of peppermint is a popular flavoring ingredient used in soaps, pharmaceuticals foods, cosmetics, and drinks. The essential oil is employed to treat analgesia, antibacterial as well as antispasmodic, anti-inflammatory and digestion, antimicrobial, and decongestive and expectorant. It helps to ease coughs.

6.Pine (Pinus Sylvestris) pinus edulis comes from the family of plants Lamiaceae and is part of the mint family. The essential oil of pine comes from the pine needles that grow on the pine trees. The smell is known for its positive, uplifting effects on mood. It's a popular cure of nausea after surgery and nausea. Essential pine oil is utilized to treat analgesia, an antibacterial as well as antibiotics, anti-infectious an anti-inflammatory, antifungal and antimicrobial drug; helping in reopening the lung and airways and as an expectorant as well as to soothe nerves.

7.Rosemary (Rosmarinus officinalis) is a member of the plant family Lamiaceae. The fragrant evergreen's primary oil is extracted from the flowering leaves, petals, and even the stems. It is a popular oil for its folk remedies, cooking food flavoring, as well as herbal tea. It is also known as a holy oil. Its uses include an analgesic, anti-inflammatory, antibacterial and antispasmodic ingredient and for breaking down mucus, as a stimulant, decongestant and expectorant as well as a muscles relaxant (cineole) and stimulant and tonic, as well as to heal wounds (verbenone).

Essential oils derived from Petal and Flowers

There are eight essential oils that are derived from flowers and petals.

1.Clary salvia (Salivia the sclarea) is a perennial herbaceous within the plant family Lamiaceae with a rich history of flowers and petals utilized as a herb. The clary essential oil sage is utilized in the manufacture of perfumes, as well as to flavor muscatel in liqueurs and wines. The essential oil can be used for its antidepressant and antifungal properties and antispasmodic. It is also anti-inflammatory and also for its aphrodisiac properties. It is used to calm the nervous system by relaxing the uterus as well as stimulating circulation of blood.

2.Chamomile (Matricaria chamomilla [Anthemis Nobilis2.Chamomile (Matricaria Chamomilla [Anthemis no) is a member of the of the family Asteraceae and is the most common term used to describe a variety of daisy-like flowers. Chamomile essential oil derived from flowers is utilized in teas made from herbal ingredients and is an extremely popular herbal tea for evening use due to its sedative effect. It is employed to help support your nervous system and can help with insomnia, inflammation as well as headaches, menstrual disorders as well as skin problems.

3.Geranium (Pelargonium and asperum) and rose (Pelargonium graveolent)--this essential oil originates from the family of plants Geraniaceae. The perennial has a fragrant floral fragrance that is used for high-end fragrances and products containing essential oils that result in youthful, radiant skin. Essential oils derived from the flower is used for relieving anxiety, acting as a sedative that helps to relax, to ease symptoms of menstrual cycle, for its anti-inflammatory properties and to support healthful lymph drainage.

4.Jasmine(Jasminum sambac, Jasminum grandiflorum)--this important oil comes part of the plant family Oleaceae. Jasmine is a genus that includes vines and shrubs that belong to the family of olives. The flowers of this bushy, strong-scented perennial are utilized for aroma and to make a base for white and green teas. Essential oil jasmine is utilized for its antidepressant properties and also as an Aphrodisiac to calm the nervous system as well for sexual stimulation as well as a stimulant.

Chapter 9: Essential Oils Derived From Rinds And Fruits

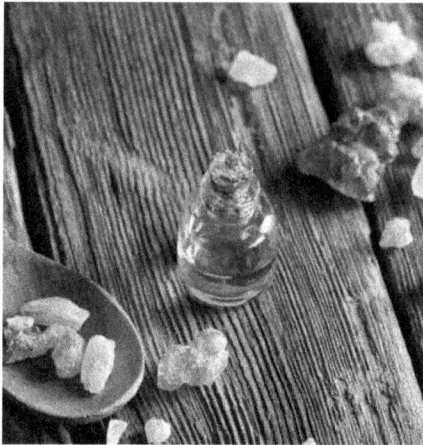

1.Bergamot (Citrus Bergamia) comes from the family of Rutaceae. The green or yellow fruit is a cross between citrus and bitter orange. It offers a bitter flavor that surpasses grapefruit however, it is not as tart as a lemon. Essential oils extracted from the zest or peel of the fruit could result in photosensitivity due to sunlight exposure damaging the skin exposed to sun. Essential oil has the scent of citrus and is used in cosmetics, perfumes, and in food items that smell. Essential oils are utilized as an air purifier and antibacterial. It is also an antidepressant Anti-inflammatory, antifungal and antiviral. They are used for relaxing and deodorizing as well as for digestion regulation (undereating or eating too much) and to reduce anxiety, acting as a tonic and sedative and to heal wounds.

2.Lemon (citrus limonum)--this vital oil is derived from the fruit of the evergreen species of a tiny tree. The oil comes from the Rutaceae plant family. It contains the skin of the fruits as well as the pulp that is used in cooking as well as non-cultural applications of the essential oil of lemon, as well as lemon pie in culinary and cleaners. A distinct, sour flavor of lemon is one of the most popular characteristics of this essential oil. The lemon essential oil can be used to treat bacterial infections as well as an anticoagulant, antidepressant Anti-infectious, antiinflammatory, antibiotic, antiviral, antioxidant, astringent and antimicrobial ingredient; an appetite stimulant, immune boost, lymphatic and digestive as well as to reduce anxiety.

3.Mandarin (Citrus Reticulatea) The essential oil made up of the Rutaceae plant family. This tiny citrus tree produces mandarin-sized oranges which are less than oranges. Mandarin is a hybrid orange is the Tangerine. The essential oil of mandarin the rind and peel is more sweet and is dried for use as a seasoning in different food products. Essential oil utilized as an analgesic antiseptic, antidepressant and the central nervous system's tonic digestive tonic, and deodorant and immune booster. It is used for decreasing anxieties and fevers, as well to help in calming.

4.Sweet orange (citrus sinensis)--this essential oil comes part of the Rutaceae plant family. The sweet, citrus-y and greenish orange oil comes taken from the zest and peel. The oil is utilized in the top perfumes. The leaves are sensitive to light but not the fruits. Sweet essential oil of orange is utilized for analgesics, antidepressants as well as antibacterial and antifungal. It is also used for an antiseptic, antiviral, deodorant and digestive tonic for relieving anxiety; an anti-stress agent; to soothe the nervous system and for stimulant use.

5.Juniper fruit (Juniperus communis)--this purple-black berry the female of evergreen cones. It is a member of the family of plants Cupressaceae which is derived from conifers. Often, it is utilized for its spice. Essential oil can be utilized as an analgesic antiseptic, antiseborrheic in addition to being anti-fungal, antiviral detoxifier, decongestant and to improve circulation and reduce fever.

Essential oils from woods and Resins

1.Cedarwood (Cedrus atlanticia)--cedarwood is from the plant family Pinaceae and the needles, leaves, bark, and wood are for extracting the essential oil. Conifers with evergreen leaves are characterized by a pleasant woodsy aroma. The essential oil is utilized to treat fungi, as a antibiotic, and as an astringent to help break down mucus and also as a calming agent and insect repellent. It also acts as a lymphatic decongestant, as well as a general tonic.

2.Frankincense (Boswellia carteri)--this vital oil comes from the family known as Burseraceae and originates from the Boswellia tree. Resin is a dried gum-like substance is utilized to make aromatic perfumes and incense. Essential oil is utilized for an antibacterial, analgesic and antidepressant. It is also an anti-infectious, antidepressant an antimicrobial and astringent as a tonic for the immune system; in reducing anxiety, for calming the mind; and to soothe the nervous system as well as the healing of wounds.

3.Sandalwood (Santalum album)--this important oil comes from the family of plants known as Santalaceae. The oil comes from wood, heartwood from the trunk as well as sawdust. The sandalwood essential oil can be found in medicine cosmetics for skin such as incense sticks, perfumes and mouthwashes. It is also used in deodorants, mouthwashes as well as antiseptics. It is an essential oil. it's utilized as an antibacterial or antidepressant. Also, it is an anti-inflammatory an antimicrobial, antiviral, and Aphrodisiac, and sedative to soothe the nervous system, and for general tonic.

Essential oils derived from Roots and Rhizomes

1.Ginger (Zingiber officinale) is extracted from roots or the rhizome, which is the plant the zingiber. Ginger is also often referred to as the oil of confidence for an increased sense of self-confidence. The oil of ginger root is one of the most frequently-used spices. Additionally, the dry and ugly root can be employed as an anti-inflammatory, diuretic, antispasmodic, antibacterial helper, boosts immunity as well as a rubefacient.

Chapter 10: What Is Aromatherapy?

You may have heard about aromatherapy in the past and you are perhaps, at the very least, familiar with the term and its meaning. The term "aromatherapy" has to do with be concerned with smells and aromas that treat ailments and diseases isn't it? It's quite amazing! Is it possible to accomplish that simply by the smell of something?

Don't worry, you're not all alone in your despair. Some have often been skeptical about the effectiveness of this approach to treatment. Is it really meant to perform? To better understand the essence of aromatherapy and its functions-- and if it is, in truth, it actually works even at all, it is necessary to gain an understanding of what it is that aromatherapy actually is.

Aromatherapy is actually the term used to describe a broad range of practices that encompasses a variety of different practices which make use of essential oils and plants in order to build an environment that is healthier, along to improve the quality of life for people. Every treatment that is currently practiced in Western civilisation that use plants and essential oils can be considered the practice of aromatherapy.

In general Aromatherapy is a kind of treatment intended for helping someone to unwind or dissociating. It is a method of treatment that uses volatile plant oils as well as essential oils in order to create physical and mental feelings. Aromatherapy generally requires aromatic ingredients created by volatile plant elements and essential oils as well as equivalent natural ingredients which are used in the form of an alternative therapy to improve an individual's health and mood.

Many of these uses make aromatherapy a well-known treatment option for alternative medicines. People who do not dislike the unpleasant side negative effects of prescription medications particularly in the case of anxiety, depression or similar conditions and other similar conditions, are choosing to make use of aromatherapy as a way to help to achieve their ideal condition of mind. It is possible to view a handful people as eccentrics in their choice to make use of aromatherapy instead of other synthetic drugs, but it's been proven to be beneficial in certain circumstances when used properly in conjunction with your medical professional.

Chapter 11: Aromatherapy History

Aromatherapy has been employed in a variety of ways since the beginning of time. In the past, people have used plant matter as well as essential oils to cure diseases or diseases. This is why it's difficult to give an exact date to the beginning of development and development of aromatherapy. The practice has changed over changing times to accommodate the unique demands of each society because the requirements of each culture changed. Also, it has changed due to new plant matter has been discovered, and essential oils were discovered and utilized.

In the context of this ever-changing world Aromatherapy, as it is as it is now has evolved through the use of distillation plant matter for the purpose of generating essential oils. This particular type of distillation is traced back to the 20th century. According to the current definitions in the field of medicine Aromatherapy is a term that was first used in the 1920s due to Renee Maurice Gattefosse, a French chemical scientist.

The well-known French scientist had dedicated his whole life to research and research related to vital oil's healing properties. His dedication was sparked by the incident that occurred on accidental accident in his lab on some time ago. Gattefosse was unable to avoid setting his arm on fire. He ran around the inside of his lab, searching for a way to put the flames. When he was looking for a barrel of liquid to put his hand into, Maurice Gattefosse came across an open container of lavender oil. The chemist quickly threw his arm in the oil of lavender to put out the flames surprise the chemist experienced almost immediate reduction in pain.

Gattefosse also discovered during this transformative experience that burned areas healed quickly and did not leave any scars. The differences between the process of healing the burns covered in lavender oil, and those burns that the chemist actually endured frequently astonished his. One of the most significant findings of the French chemical chemist made was the fact that lavender oil was actually reducing the time to heal, with no swelling, soreness or scarring.

It wasn't until after the Second World War that the study of Jean Valnet French scientist were carried out through Jean Valnet's research. Jean Valnet had actually utilized essential oils as well as other distillate plant substances to deal the gangrene problem in wounded soldiers. Although it wasn't always the best option but there were many occasions when Jean Valnet was able of saving lives of soldiers by using essential oils-which proved to be a valuable knowledge during wartime crises.

Chapter 12: Is Aromatherapy Worth The Time?

It is a common issue for the vast majority of people who are thinking of aromatherapy. Is aromatherapy actually effective, or is it just untrue? There is a common mistaken notion that aromatherapy is a new concept. Aromatherapy has been around alive and recognized as such for around the past 80 years. However, the fundamental nature of aromatherapy is actually present since the beginning of time.

In the beginning, don't be fooled by companies that will try to market their scented items as products for aromatherapy. There are some businesses that exaggerate unsubstantiated claims in order to increase revenue. In countries such as the US the aromatherapy industry is considered as an additional chemical and the FCC requires a proper identification of every component. Be sure the item you're looking at contains real components and not manufactured ones.

What about serious illnesses? Do aromatherapy treatments actually help mental or physical health problems? In reality, aromatherapy is not able to relieve the stress of a condition. Anyone who makes an attempt to use aromatherapy to cure some issue will not be satisfied. It's not how aromatherapy works.

But, it is designed for helping you deal with the physical symptoms, any signs of medical issue, improve your mood and help relieve stress or aid in other psychological issues. However, this doesn't mean the signs and issues will disappear. Aromatherapy could help make these issues and signs easier to manage.

Aromatherapy can't treat cancer AIDS and other important health conditions. Instead, it aids in relieving anxiety of anxiety, reducing the feeling of queasiness as well as improving an individual's overall mood. This should never be considered as the primary method of treatment for a serious medical issue. It is merely the basis for a complement to various other therapies that are in progress.

The possibility exists of substituting the use of prescription drugs or other non-prescription chemicals for specific areas. In particular, it can give you a significant benefit in dealing with indigestion, swelling, injuries as well as psychological and emotional issues.

Furthermore, aromatherapy isn't likely to be the same to every person who tries it. The sensory memories you have will influence the extent to which treatment can benefit you. This is why that if you experience dissatisfaction with one particular aspect it is unlikely bring about the results you desire.

Chapter 13: Aromatherapy At Home

Aromatherapy is treatment methods or as a way to prevent certain diseases which can prove very beneficial in reducing stress levels. Essential oils released through aromatherapy can are extremely beneficial to the center of the smell brain specifically on the limbic region. Although no specific medical research studies have proven positive results of aromatherapy for the body, many initial research-based studies suggest the synergy between our processes of healing the body and aromatic essential oils. Aromatherapy is often released in the form of gas or vapor in aromatherapy. The essential oils are often burned.

In the English-speaking world Aromatherapy is used every day regardless of whether you're unfamiliar with the term. A lot of people who live in Western cultures may not consider it an aromatherapy but it is very likely that they will encounter it every day by using massage oils, fragrances and scented creams. That's one reason to which a lot of experts tend to emphasize the use of aromatherapy through candles and massage oils. Only in America as well as other countries that speak English where aromatherapy is seen as an alternative method of treatment.

Have you ever used fragrances to create your preferred scent? Are you familiar with creams which, in some way, just feel so soothing to you? Have you ever lit incense bearing names such as "Tranquility," and discovered that the scent was soothing, as was the aid to the process of unwinding?

All of these are elements of aromatherapy, in a complementar sense. These are all methods that make use of aromas or scents as well as others natural ingredients to help in creating a soothing welcoming, warm and comfortable atmosphere.

In France in the region the country where it first came to be discovered and practiced, aromatherapy is part of their national standard medicine. In France the country, there's a concentration on the many advantages of essential oils such as antibacterial, antiviral antibiotic, and anti-bacterial properties. There is a possibility that the same qualities present in other distillate plant substances and apply these characteristics in order to control the spread of infection. This differs from methods that are common to the majority of countries that speak English. In France and the countries that surround it there is a common practice to have a patient given essential oils that can be administered by a physician.

Can you imagine what it is similar to for you in the US? Imagine going to a physician who gave the aromatherapy treatment to relieve anxiety, rather than synthetic medication. This is a far cry from the standard treatments we're used to receiving in our Western world. However, many other countries make use of aromatherapy remedies to fight off diseases and combat existing health conditions or ailments.

While there have many discoveries made in the field of aromatherapy the modern day aromatherapy practice is type of scientific field, but it has not been verified by any of the US, Germany, Russia and Japan. It's common to see doctors in these countries not to recognize the benefits of aromatherapy therapies. However, many countries around the globe continue to use aromatherapy to treat ailments and diseases, and also to stop the spread of illnesses, diseases as well as illnesses. In spite of the obvious efficacy of aromatherapy and its ability to reduce stress levels, the vast majority of doctors from Western societies aren't keen using aromatherapy to deal anxiety.

Chapter 14: Aromatherapy And The Limbic System?

Perhaps the benefits of aromatherapy may not be as apparent to you. It's helpful to know the way aromatherapy works to know what it does to help. Aromatherapy's primary effects affect the brain's limbic system. This system of the limbic has been described by doctors as a series of brain structures, which support many tasks. The brain's functions that the limbic system performs include memory and movement functions. This system of the brain works together with the autonomic nervous system and the endocrine. In the endocrine systems, the limbic system can be able to influence the pleasure that can be felt. This same part of the brain plays a role in sexual stimulation, in addition to other instances of high endorphin.

Because of the significant role of a scent in creating specific experiences or emotions it could prove to prove to be an effective tool used for treating the limbic system of the brain.

There are various aromatherapy scents along with the associated feelings to these aromas. They are designed in order to remind people of an enjoyable time or event within the lives of the person. The limbic system's reaction to the scent is one reason why many aromatherapy items are able to achieve some results by using fragrances that have a seasonal theme. At times, the scent of the candles that smell of cinnamon can bring back memories of Christmas.

Have you ever wondered what triggers your of specific places, people or even things? Have you noticed that certain scents can create a feeling of warmth and comfortable and bring you back of locations in which you felt happy, whereas others could produce an opposite effect? It's a lot like what aromatherapy does. Aromas and scents can trigger certain bodily reactions that produce an effect that is desired.

Chapter 15: Essential Oils

Choosing the Best Essential Oils

Many essential oils can be used for aromatherapy. There's at minimum 90 essential oils, and fifteen carrier oils commonly utilized for aromatherapy. With a variety of different oils to pick from, it's no wonder that a majority of people struggle to determine which oils are suitable to suit their needs. It's essential to research the different kinds of oils and determine which will be ideal to use, in the event that you decide to use aromatherapy.

Essential oils undiluted as well as similar products that are suitable for aromatherapy can typically be distinguished from equivalent products because, most of the time, oil that is not diluted have a therapeutic grade. Naturally, this is only a basis to base your decisions on when you live in a country that regulates the marketplace. In the US there is a standardization of the contents of the oils' components is standardized to meet the requirements of FCC labels. FCC labeling defines the codex of food chemicals, it's a standard that was developed by the FCC which defines the amounts of each fragrance.

This type of law can be used to aid in the process of regulating the market, so that aromatherapy is at least a semblance to guidelines. The FCC help in the regulation of aromatherapy but also in identifying the types of plants and essential oils work best to use in certain therapies. In addition, the regulations define exactly how much of each oil needs to be employed to fulfill a specific purpose eliminating concerns about using too much of an oil. The law does not restricts the use of synthetic chemicals in order to satisfy the standards set by the FCC in relation to a specific oil.

The best approach in determining whether an essential oil can prove useful is to use a trained nose. Many those who are knowledgeable in aromatherapy will often discern if the scent is a fake or natural. It is a skill that is thought to be available to anyone in the event that one is willing to put in the time and effort. You must stay away from adulterated products and essential oils that you use to enhance your Aromatherapy as often as you can.

Whatever scent, therapy or treatment that you decide to go with however, it's essential that you remain true to your preferred choice. Many times when you love the way the oil feels or smells, you'll most likely appreciate using the product. If you aren't enthralled with the aroma and feel of the oil, it's unlikely make any difference no matter what this particular scent or oil can accomplish or the way it is supposed assist you. If you're not enjoying the scent of an essential oil, it is your body's way of encouraging you to continue searching.

Evaluating Essential Oils

If you're out in the field exploring various essential oils to use in your aromatherapy, make sure that you test the oil in the right way. For a sample, simply let the bottle sit for 3 or 4 inches right under your nose. Slowly sway the bottle left to right as you inhale slowly. It is important to not breath in too deep or use the bottle as an inhaler. Inhaling the fragrance more in depth will not increase the efficacy and could be dangerous as specific oils can have strong scents.

By this process through this tasting, you should be able to determine the oils that feel natural to you and which oils trigger particular feelings within your body. In the past, I have mentioned often, people associate the scent of cinnamon to the holidays The same could be said for the smell of pine trees and campfires. There isn't an essential oil to campfires, there are essential oils the pine tree scent and almost any other season or event you want to evoke.

Explaining Essential Oils?

Essential oil is typically an oil that has been harvested from a plant, and then distilled. The distillation process typically consists of water derived from a river or slow-moving river, mingled with flowers, leaves branches, bark, and various other elements of the plant used to create this particular oil. Essential oils aren't really make you feel oily at all in contrast to the term. Most essential oils are crystal clear or appear to be an extremely transparent colour, such as orange or amber. Essential oils are believed to contain the actual essence of the tree or plant of which they are derived. Due to the large amount of essential oils the essential oils are usually available in small bottles that can last for quite a long period of time.

Essential oils, even though they are fragrances, are not the same or even like aromas or fragrances. Essential oils are produced from real plants unlike the vast majority of fragrance or perfume oils are made from synthetic materials or comprise chemical compounds that have very little or no benefit to healing. Because the term "aromatherapy" is not yet controlled through authorities of the US the federal authorities, a lot of firms are likely to employ aromatic oils to treat ailments. oils, even though they're different from each other. It is an unfortunate situation because often the aromatherapy oils contain very little or no natural ingredients. It is important to understand that if an item for aromatherapy contains any type of synthetic or fragrance oil, it's not really an aromatherapy product. There is merely a bid to promote a less expensive product as superior.

The chemical composition and scent of the essential oils that are restorative is what makes them so effective. Aroma and chemical makeup are able to provide important physical benefits as well as emotional relaxation. The majority of people who try oil-based remedies do it through methods that involve applying diluted oils onto the skin or inhaling.

The Main Essential Oils

There are a variety of essential oils and they all have distinct characteristics. It's possible that you don't even know that, yet some of these oils are used in different types in cooking! A few of these essential oils can be found when cooking for your family with a different format (like ground powder, or leaves):

Basil

Basil is commonly used to cook for a variety of purposes because of its unique flavor. Its aroma is herbal, licorice-like and sweet. Although Basil is often used for cooking, it is also used to help ailments like bronchitis, colds or coughs, inflame, fatigue bug bites as well as gout, insect repellent and muscle pains as well as sinus issues, and the rheumatic disease. However, it is advised to only use basil in small amounts and cautiously. In excess, Basil could cause cancer since it is a source of the chemical methyl chloravicol. It is suggested to avoid using basil if you are suffering from liver disorders, and that it is recommended to refrain of using it during your the pregnancy.

Ginger

It is often used to cook, is an additional essential oil for aromatherapy. It is a hot warmth, woodsy, and earthy odor. Ginger is an ideal remedy to treat muscle pain, arthritis as well as queasiness and poor blood circulation. However, it is not recommended to make use of this remedy if you're likely to be in intense sunlight for an extended amount of time because it may cause sun-related poisoning.

Lemon

Lemon is a very common fruit that most people know about. Its aroma is comparable to the scent of the rinds of a lemon. But, it's more intense and more powerful. It can be used for treating colds, athlete's foot, chilblains, dull skin spots, flu, corns as well as warts and varicose blood vessels. Like Ginger and Ginger, it's recommended to avoid lemon if you will expose yourself to sunlight over a long period of duration.

Parsley

Parsley is also used for cooking. It's got a very smell that is woodsy and quite appealing. It's typically used to treat cellsulites, amenorrhea and arthritis as well as cystitis, frigidity stomach pain as well as rheumatism and dangerous accumulation. But, this essential oil could sometimes pose a risk. The oil is believed to cause poisoning to the liver, and may trigger abortions. This should be used in a cautious manner, particularly when pregnant women are involved.

Peppermint

Peppermint is a very common smell that you're likely familiar with. It smells minty and very similar to spearmint only more powerful and sweet. Its scent is likely to often remind people of the Christmas season. It's a great treatment for asthma, colic and other respiratory conditions, such as fever, fatigue, nausea, headache, flatulence as well as scabies, vertigo and sinus issues. The scabies can poison the nerves, and should be not be taken when someone is afflicted by epilepsy or fever. Peppermint can be taken by mouth, however only under the supervision by a qualified aromatherapy expert.

Thyme

The herb is often used for cooking. It's got a pleasant, yet herbal smell. It is often used for combating arthritis, colds and dermatitis. It is also used to treat cuts, insects, flu muscles, laryngitis and lice, poor circulatory system, oily skin the aching throat, and scabies. Patients who suffer from high blood pressure should be cautious when using the herb. It can cause inflammation, or cause a severe mucous membrane irritating.

Rose

Particularly intriguing is the use of Rose as an aromatherapy. Everyone is familiar with the idea of using roses for gifts. But, they can also be employed to treat the smell. They possess a sweet and flowery scent. In its most essential oil type can be used for treating eczema stress, wrinkles and menopausal symptoms, as well as frigidity and anxiety. If you are thinking of gifting roses to someone you admire take note that the scent of roses may aid in relieving stress and anxiety. This is why women appreciate them greatly.

Nutmeg

We all know about the nutmeg. It's a fantastic aroma that is abounding and spicy. It is also fragrant and woody. Its essential oil is similar to cooking spices, only much more fragrant and richer. The most common use for it is to treat constipation as well as muscle pains fatigue, queasyness poor blood circulation nerve pain, rheumatism and slow digestion of food.

Marjoram

Marjoram is also a culinary spice, but it is not used as frequently as the other spices mentioned here. When it comes to aromatherapy it's woody delicious scent can be appealing. It can manage a wide range of problems while pleasant to smell. It can be used to treat the effects of amenorrhea, achy muscles, chilblains, asthma and colic, excessive libido as well as coughing up, the high blood pressure, flatulence muscular cramps, neuralgia tension, rheumatism, sprains or ticks and even stress. However, pregnant women ought be cautious about using the drug, even if there aren't any other security measures.

Lavender

In the past, during the time of aromatherapy, there was discussion about how the French chemical chemist Gattefosse came across the aromatherapy method by experimenting with a dosage that contained Lavender oil. What exactly does Lavender really tackle? Its refreshing, sweet fragrant, floral and refreshing scent is a favorite. It can be utilized for allergies such as acne, asthma and anxiety, as well as athlete's foot burns, bruises cuts, chickenpox and dysmenorrhea. It can also be used to treat cystitis, dys flatulence and earache. It can also be used to treat high blood pressure and insect bites headaches, itching, insect repellants and labor pains. It can also be used to treat headaches, oily skin, migraines as well as rheumatism and scars. scabies, strains, sprains or sores, stretch marks as well as stress, whooping cold and vertigo. With all the different treatment options, there's not a necessity for safety precautions with this oil.

Essential Oil Safety

Similar to all medicines, treatments as well as treatments that you can avail, it is vital to practice caution and care while using essential oils. Be aware that they highly concentrated liquids which could cause harm in the event that they aren't used properly or used in an appropriate manner. However, don't allow that to scare you. As it is that you are able to practice proper the right way and are well-informed that you will be well with aromatherapy.

Although certain safety guidelines must be followed however, these standards can be violated under the supervision by a trained and certified aromatherapy expert in the case of specific aromatherapy oils. In case you're unsure, check with your physician or a accredited and qualified aromatherapy specialist.

One important thing to keep in mind is the fact that an essential oil shouldn't be applied undiluted to the skin. There are some instances where this is not the case however, it is not recommended to take a decision with no careful assessment by an expert in the field. The application of the oil on your skin may cause skin reactions, such as rashes, or hypersensitivity which could prove to be very dangerous. Tea tree and lavender can be applied to the skin but it is only to be done at very limited times to ensure that you don't be at risk of sensitivity.

Keep in mind that specific oils may trigger allergies or sensitivities for individuals. Similar to many items, some people have a tendency to react to essential oils used in aromatherapy. In order to protect yourself as well as others from potential allergy, you should always put small amounts of dilute essential oils (never ever not diluted) on a small area of the skin. It is possible to apply the oil to your elbow's insides, and afterwards apply a band-aid. The oil should be left to rest for at minimum a week for a test to see if it causes any reaction. There is no need to think you aren't affected by an essential oil but you should keep checking from the beginning.

Certain essential oils can also be a problem during pregnancy, or those suffering from asthma, epilepsy or other health problems. Be aware of this and seek out precautions for that oil before using it in conjunction with a person who is prone to developing a medical condition to prevent any issues.

Do not use essential oils in a way other than following specific directions by a physician or certified aromatherapy specialist. Certain oils cannot be consumed orally. However, it is rare to find people who could do it, but specifically, in controlled doses. They should only be ordered by a doctor or a certified aromatherapy expert.

Contrary to many items the essential oils keep following the rule of smaller is better. Use only a small amount of essential oils enough to complete the task. Essential oils are highly concentrated and are very easy to apply over.

It is not all that can be considered an essential oil should be used for aromatherapy. Particular essential oils, such as pennyroyal, wormwood and horseradish. Camphor, wintergreen, sassafras and bitter almond need be only used with the advice of trained aromatherapists in the event that it is employed in any way.

Keep in mind that essential oils are fire-proof! Always keep essential oils away from dangers of fire, and be sure to use extreme caution in the event that your oils come close to the flames.

It goes with the idea that you should not allow children to use essential oils in the absence of an adult who is familiar with aromatherapy. However, it is possible to not be mindful of the safety precautions by preventing children from being able to go into the store for essential oils. Make sure they are safe far from the reach of children.

Dangerous Oils

Certain oils are considered to be harmful and hazardous. However, just because the oil is not categorized as hazardous, that does not mean it's safe or doesn't have any other adverse consequences that you should be conscious of. Be sure to study the essential oils before using the oils.

Chapter 16: Remaining Safe

Do you have the ability to use aromatherapy for your pets?

As aromatherapy is good for us but it is also beneficial for our pets by providing pets with the needed recuperation. But, it's crucial to keep in mind that animals aren't exactly identical to humans. It is best to talk to a qualified aromatherapy expert who is familiar with animals. One of the best books on this issue includes "Holistic Aromatherapy for Animals" written by Kristen Leigh Bell, 2002. The guide is the sole important source about the effects of aromatherapy on animals.

Aromatherapy and Kids?

If you are planning to use aromatherapy for your children take note that the majority of recipes and guidelines currently available for aromatherapy are intended for healthy and average-sized adults who are under the supervision by a physician. The recipes that are intended for children must have a lesser amount than that typically needed. Certain oils should not be administered to children for any reason. It is best to be mindful in these situations It is essential to always take safety precautions and be cautious when you use Aromatherapy with your children.

Certain oils that are acceptable for kids even in tiny doses include rose, neroli tea tree citrus, roman chamomile, and lavender. Children must be given specific needs based on the size, age, requirements and weight. Hence, it's best to talk with a licensed professional in this area.

Aromatherapy and Pregnant Women?

It is a very popular topic. There are many who do not think the need to use aromatherapy used with women who are pregnant because possible side effects can go not always identified however there is a lack of will to "check" this out to determine if the fetuses are likely be impacted through aromatherapy in a detrimental in any way. There are some who claim that specific essential oils can be utilized but it's not possible to conclude that specific essential oils should never be employed by a female.

Certain essential oils may trigger the uterus to contract or even spontaneous abortions. Certain oils can cause problems because they can be harmful to diabetics, and many pregnant women will to develop diabetes in the course of pregnancy. There is no way to tell, however that these oils are used correctly and in a safe manner at the time of the incidents.

Much of the study is actually carried out in animals since it's dangerous to perform the same type of test on human beings. However, scientists have discovered some essential oils known as causing problems during the pregnancy. This includes:

Bergamot

Benzoin

Lavender

Grapefruit

Neroli

Lemon

Patchouli

Orange

Spearmint

Sandalwood

Tea Tree

Vetiver

Beware of these products if you're expecting or in danger of becoming pregnant. It's better to find alternatives to avoid the risk and avoid regret when you get older.

Chapter 17: Carrier Oils

What are Carrier Oils?

Carrier oils can be another component of treatment for aromatherapy. Although they're typically thought of as vegetable oils or base oils, they serve a wider purpose. Carrier oils can be used to break down the essential oils and CO_2's and even absolutes before applying them to the skin. You can take an essential oil that has been diluted and mix it up with a carrier oil, or base oil. It will be considered to be reduced. This will make the process safe for you to apply it to the skin.

Different carrier oils have different varieties of characteristics and offer healing properties on their own, or increase the healing benefits of the essential oil that you're using. They're typically made from the cold-pressing of vegetable oils, which are produced from the fatty components of certain plant species. They are not volatile or impart their unique scent to essential oils. It is interesting to note that carrier oils may become stale. Although essential oils can be used for a long time, common carrier oils can expire. Your goal is for your carriers oils to be organic or have vitamin E. It is used as a preservative.

How to Use Different Kinds of Carrier Oils?

There are a variety of carriers oils. Here are a few the most commonly used carrier oils.

Olive oil

Olive oil is usually used in cooking. The scent it has is similar to the oil used in cooking. By this, I mean that it smells similar to olives. The texture is thick and a little oily. Additionally, it is mild to medium-green color. It's important to use a small amount or an appropriate amount in diluting as it could overpower the blend.

Peanut oil

The oil of peanut has a remarkably delicate scent, with a mildly sweet nutty flavor. The texture is a bit thick and creates an extremely oily layer on your skin. Its hue is nearly clear.

Use care when using peanut oil since it should not be applied to anyone with an allergy to peanuts. It's usually a great alternative to use along with massage oils or as the form of a mix for massage due to its oily appearance as well as its ability to help arthritis sufferers.

Sweet Almond oil

Sweet almond oil smells mild and slightly nutty sweet aroma. It's slightly oily, and can create an oily feel to the skin. However it absorbed rapidly. It's essentially transparent with a yellowish tint. Sweet almond oil can be a diverse carrier oil that could be combined with almost every essential oil. Additionally, it's affordable making it a great choice for the vast most essential oils.

Cocoa Butter Oil

Cocoa butter oil comes with an intense and sweet aroma that definitely smells like chocolate. It is robust and durable at the temperature of room and can break into small pieces. However, it's excellent for heating and relieving at a cool or cool temperature. The color is a little brown. Cocoa butter oil must be blended with other items or oils to use it. It's an excellent oil that can be mixed into lotions and creams.

Hazelnut Oil

Hazelnut oil is mild, nutty but sweet smell. It's light and leaves an oily, slightly sour feeling. It's particularly good to use for those who suffer from oily skin because it isn't able to leave the same oily residue like other oils. The absence of a oily residue suggests that people using it will not suffer from breakouts often, which affects an enormous portion of people in the USA worldwide due to oil content and the oil residue left behind by products.

Pecan Oil

Pecan oil is a light fragrant and rich scent. It is medium in thickness, leaving only an oily layer over the face. The color is nearly clear but it is believed that it is prone to spoiling quite quickly. It must be stored in a dark colored bottle and kept in a dark area in order to keep the bottle from sun exposure that could make it deteriorate.

There are a variety of different carrier oils can be used each with distinct functions, aroma or color, as well as texture. The list below isn't comprehensive but it will give you a good idea of possible oils are a good option in order to dilute essential oils.

Chapter 18: Other Materials

Absolutes

Absolutes have a lot in common with essential oils. They're extremely aromatic fluids and have been extracted by removing plant materials. However, the difference between essential oils and absolutes is that essential oils are extracted using an extremely complex method. This requires chemical solvents that will need be extracted in the final stages of the production.

Absolutes are known to be stronger in comparison to essential oils. This is the reason why it's vital to incorporate essential oils to heal yourself to treat yourself when you use aromatherapy to treat a medical condition or a method to ease tension.

The main drawback to using absolutes, or developing absolutes, is that it could result in small amounts of trace elements remaining from the chemical solvent within the final product. This is not able to be solved, because there's no way to know if all the solvents were actually gotten off of the product prior to reaching the final stages of project. That is the reason why a lot of people use absolutes only in a limited way since they're not 100% organic, as they have to be dragged through chemicals.

The other major distinction in absolutes versus essential oils is the fact that, with essential oils, it's not recommended that they be consumed internally unless with the help of someone who has been skilled, knowledgeable and educated sufficient to make the appropriate choice. But, it is much more extreme in the case of absolutes that should never take internally regardless of the person you are. The chemical trace within the absolutes is a guarantee of this.

Hydrosols

Hydrosols is another ingredient that can be used in aromatherapy therapies. They are the water molecules that remain after removing essential oils from plant materials. It is often referred to as the distillate or the floral water.

In the process of extracting essential oils from plant matter The water is bound be infused with the amazing scent as well as many of the restorative properties of the oil. But, hydrosols are merely byproducts from the process of distillation.

Resins

It is possible that you have heard the term resins. Resin is an organic compound which is naturally formed when the tree is damaged. When the bark is cut the trees will create a tough, dense and sticky substance that's called resin. The resin can be used for various purposes including making toys or other items that collect value.

Natural resins derived from trees are believed to have healing effects. But, it is difficult to work with the resins because of their sticky and dense nature. The liquid types of resin can be identified that have been extracted using an method of solvent extraction or alcohol.

CO2s

CO2s are the oils that have successfully extracted using an innovative method. The method involves the carbon dioxide. Carbon dioxide is compressed until it is an oil. It is then used to dissolve the natural plant matter as the plant material which would then formed essential oil, is dissolved into CO2 liquid. Then, the CO2 mixture gets re-drawn back to its original state and CO2 particles are dissolved to form a gaseous state and leave the oil that is formed.

The majority of the time, CO2s are considered to be identical to essential oils because of the fact that there's absolutely no evidence toxic chemical or solvent product. This doesn't diminish the potency of the oil. CO2s typically are more robust and resemble the scent that comes from the plant material that was used to create them. CO2s are often regarded as an excellent product.

Infused Oils

A different kind of oil that is commonly used in aromatherapy is known as an infused oil. Infused oil employs a specific method to extract the essential oils of plant materials. This method of extraction, the carrier oil is infused by various herbs. This type of oil has all the characteristics of a carrier oil but is also infused with healing properties from both the oil and herbs that are infused into the oil.

Although many plants possess the ability to heal or recover However, not all species can transform to essential oils. The reason is that they lack sufficient oil content for it to be extracted in order to create essential oil. This is the reason the reason why you should infuse that particular herb or plant using the help of a carrier oil in order to produce an oil that is infused.

Chapter 19: Aromatherapy For Psychological Wellness

The use of aromatherapy, particularly when it is combined with essential oils, is extremely beneficial to promote strong emotional well-being. Aromatherapy can help in the promotion of positive emotions, and may assist in overcoming issues such as sorrow and anger or even disappointment. Anyone who is stressed each day should think about applying essential oils every day to aid in creating a calmer atmosphere to ease their stress.

The reason aromatherapy works efficiently in this situation is because essential oils are composed of chemical compounds that are naturally present in plant matter, and can be absorbed as a synergy. The molecules they contain are easily breathed through, which makes them able to work quickly and get quickly absorbed into the body.

Aromatherapy's molecules can stimulate and affect the brain. The triggers it delivers to the brain may trigger certain kinds of emotions and can also mask different types of emotions. Of course, not all essential oils will be equally beneficial to everyone. Additional memories linked to certain types of scents could affect how the smell will affect an individual's mood.

In other words, if you experience a particularly strong mental reaction to one particular scent or type of oil it will affect its ability to influence your mental health positively. When cinnamon, typically an uplifting and comforting scent is actually being linked to the death of someone in your family, you're likely to not be positively in the direction of cinnamon.

What essential oils should you use to improve your mental health?

There is a belief among those who practice aromatherapy that it can greatly affect and enhance the psychological health of an individual. As humans, we have a variety of emotions. We must be aware of these emotions to be able to continue functioning in the world. It can be difficult to manage others when you are afflicted with sadness. It is much more so when you are afflicted by anger.

That's why a few users rely on aromatherapy for way to manage the intense emotions. Certain oils contain qualities that can handle a variety of feelings.

The following list will cover most our human emotions, which we would like to control or enhance.

Anger

Jasmine, Bergamot, Orange, Neroli, Petitgrain, Patchouli, Roman Chamomile, Vetiver, Rose, Ylang Ylang

Anxiety

Cedarwood, Bergamot, Frankincense, Clary Sage, Lavender, Geranium, Mandarin, Patchouli, Neroli, Roman Chamomile, Sandalwood, Rose, Vetiver

Self-confidence

Bergamot, Bay Laurel, Grapefruit, Cypress, Orange, Jasmine, Rosemary

Depression

Clary Sage, Bergamot, Geranium, Frankincense, Helichrysum, Grapefruit, Jasmine, Lemon, Lavender, Mandarin, Orange, Neroli, Roman Chamomile, Sandalwood, Rose, Ylang Ylang

Tiredness, Fatigue and Burnout

Bergamot, Basil, Black Pepper, Cypress, Frankincense, Clary Sage, Ginger, Grapefruit, Jasmine, Lemon, Helichrysum, Patchouli, Peppermint, Sandalwood, Rosemary, Vetiver

Fear

Cedarwood, Bergamot, Clary Sage, Grapefruit, Frankincense, Lemon, Jasmine, Neroli, Roman Chamomile, Orange, Sandalwood, Vetiver

Grief

Frankincense, Cypress, Helichrysum, Rose, Neroli, Sandalwood, Vetiver

Happiness and Peace

Frankincense, Bergamot, Geranium, Lemon, Grapefruit, Orange, Neroli, Rose, Ylang Ylang, Sandalwood

Insecurity

Cedarwood, Bergamot, Frankincense, Sandalwood, Jasmine, Vetiver

Irritability

Mandarin, Lavender, Roman Chamomile, Neroli, Sandalwood

Loneliness

Clary Sage, Bergamot, Frankincense, Roman Chamomile, Helichrysum, Rose

Memory and Concentration

Black Pepper, Basil, Cypress, Lemon, Hyssop, Rosemary, Peppermint

Panic and Panic Attacks

Helichrysum, Frankincense, Lavender, Rose, Neroli

Stress

Bergamot, Benzoin, Clary Sage, Geranium, Grapefruit, Frankincense, Jasmine, Mandarin, Lavender, Neroli, Patchouli, Rose, Roman Chamomile, Sandalwood, Ylang Ylang, Vetiver

Can Aromatherapy Aid With Depression?

Most of the time depression is caused through chemical or hormonal imbalances, or by triggers that are triggered by situations. The most common "situational" trigger could be the death of a loved one in the family as well as physical or verbal abuse or physical assault, financial challenges, relocation lonely, retiring, unemployment, divorce or pressure from life. In the majority of cases who suffer from depression, it is a short-term issue and is a quick-fix. Some depressions may last longer.

If you believe you are suffering from depression, it's recommended to consult an experienced doctor in order to listen to the issues. They will likely advise you to seek treatment and may require you start taking medication. It's recommended to deal with depression in the direction of a medical professional.

If you opt to employ aromatherapy for your depression, bear at heart that it's only a supplement to. Aromatherapy may be extremely beneficial for improving your general mood and perspective, but it's not a substitute for treatment options to treat your depression, particularly those who are triggered due to hormonal or chemical imbalances.

Chapter 20: Aromatherapy And Weight Loss?

Aromatherapy is an highly popular topic in relation to losing weight. As everyone is looking for an easy solution to weight issues, every chance has been devoted towards a possible method to lose weight. Like all aspects of aromatherapy there has already been a certain amount of results, however it is dependent on the variables.

Similar to all other weight loss strategies should be sought the advice of a physician or other professional before you begin any strategy for losing weight. It's best to partner with a professional who is knowledgeable in this area to make sure that the strategy you choose be created that clearly meets your specific needs.

Of course, using essential oils won't be enough result in losing weight in a shocking manner. Aromatherapy, however, can aid in lessening the desire to eat. This is by lessening the craving for food and reducing the desire to consume more. Additionally, it can assist by providing more energy while you exercise and reduce the fatigue to make you are more inclined to get up and go for a run.

A weight loss plan requires right foods and doing lots of exercise. Be sure to keep this in mind while creating your personal fitness plan since it's important to adhere to the same schedule to lose the weight. The other items that you include in your strategy are only meant to help you work toward your goal.

Chapter 21: Mixing Essential Oils

A unique and fascinating aspect that essential oils have is the fact that they can be combined to trigger specific responses in people who are exposed to the oil. It is easy to create your own essential oil blend for a beautiful, aromatic mix to your personal satisfaction and to help with fragrancing the room. Essential oils may also be combined to aid in easing muscle tension, decreasing anxiety, and enhancing joy. There are two primary reasons to mix essential oils: Therapeutic and aromatic.

In the case of aromatic blends The focus is on the smell of the finished product. Certain aromatic blends will have beneficial effects, the focus is on creating a specific sort of smell or scent to serve a particular purpose. Natural components should only be used, such as absolutes, grains alcohol, carrier oils and water. Other essential oils or herbs.

Most people are working to make a certain scent that is woodsy, hot, earthy, flowery and minty medicinal, spicy, or Oriental scent. Be sure to check the aroma qualities in the oil that you use to make sure that they don't compete with one another too much. It can also provide a good way to determine which essential oils are minty hot, or woodsy.

However, you don't need to stick to the same type or quality of scent to make a stunning collection. As an example, Oriental and spicy oils tend to work very well with Orientals, citrus or floral oils if they're not overpowering. Flowers tend to blend well with citrus as well as spicy and woodsy oils. Keep this in mind while you make the mix of oils since these oils could help you relax more and give you better treatments. Many mixes can be used. In order to determine which one of the above works best for you it's best to study a range of aromatherapy products before you decide which is the best for you.

When it comes to these blends, the main focus is on the therapeutic effect of the mixture. The blends are designed for the treatment of an emotional or physical issue. It is recommended to blend oils with beneficial uses (like dealing with asthma). It is possible to mix a variety of essential oils, that are recommended as a way to deal asthma. The mixture should not be used as a routine therapy for treating asthma. If you are experiencing the symptoms of asthma, it's essential to use an inhaler for the first step in treatment, along with aromatherapy. It is designed aid in cooling an asthma attack as well as preventing attacks of asthma.

It is also possible to mix essential oils that possess diverse properties in order to treat something similar to the combination of asthma or high blood pressure sleeplessness and arthritis. Make sure to not combine it with other kinds of essential oils that could cause harm to your health. Also, be vigilant if pregnant or suffer from an allergy to peanuts.

Be aware that some essential oils can be stimulating in contrast to other essential oils that are likely cause drowsiness. If you intend to apply the oil prior to start of the day be sure to avoid using essential oils that are likely to induce you to go to doze off. It also works the reverse, therefore make sure you don't use any stimulating oils before you go to bed because this can cause the person to stay awake throughout the evening, and make you feel not enough rested to return to your job as an energetic and effective person.

Blending the oils in order to address diverse ailments is an excellent solution to your problems. Take care when you mix your mixtures and avoid using too much of any overpowering type of oil that could cause it to be difficult for you to feel how the different oils.

What is the best way to mix?

There is no standard recommendations to mix essential oils in such a way that you can create a particular scent or healing mix. There are however crucial tips you be thinking about while you're mixing the oils you use. The best way to begin is with a small amount of drops of any sort of oil because smaller amounts are going aid you in not over-using any oil. This will also aid you in determining whether more is better or if less is more, and decide which will be the best one for your situation.

The first step is to start the mix by using only essential oils, CO2s, or absolutes. Then, you can make it a little more diluted with alcohol or another carrier oil when you need to. It's will help you avoid having to throw away any carriers or alcohol. Be sure to keep the exact details of each oil you're using along with the various drops that are used to make that particular oil. It's too easy to lose track of time and not take note of those meticulous notes. However you'll need these notes to recreate your process at a later time or when you want to do the ability to duplicate it.

Label each mix with care to ensure you are aware of exactly what's in they, what they are used for and what's within the mix. It is also possible to think of applying a different identity to the mix.

You must be cautious in the use of oil that has a powerful fragrance. Certain scents can be more potent than others, and may overwhelm others when not used with the right blend. It is possible to think of experimenting with these oils prior to mixing them with other scents so that you can determine the strength of the scent and what its effect might be.

Although you may not enjoy your music right away It's not the best idea to ruin the mix. Keep the mixture for a few days and then revisit it in the future. Sometimes, the ingredients in your blend may need to be settled and create an appropriate aroma. Additionally, you could become accustomed to the scent! Additionally, you may have been exposed to many intense scents prior the "questionable" item becoming complete and making it difficult to feel a strong sense of the smell.

Chapter 22: Diffusers

A diffuser is a tool that you can use for aiding in dispersing essential oil molecules in the air. It allows you to optimally benefit from aromatherapy treatments when you breathe in your normal air.

Tissues

The most simple method of diffusion is through a handkerchief or tissue. The tissue contains a lot of tiny drops of oil that are sprayed on it However, the tissue will carry the molecules wherever you use the tissue. It's incredibly lightweight and is able to be placed in the pocket of your bag and carried around to work with you discreet and easy to carry.

Steam Diffusion

Steam diffusion is another method. It is possible to boil several cups of water before putting them in the bowl. Many oil drops will need to be placed in the bowl. It is true that boiling water is likely to stop it launching steam up into the air. However, the steam is now going to be carrying essential oils in it. This can be a relaxing method of attempting to use Aromatherapy as it could be the perfect complement to a massage or spa service.

Candle diffusion

If you do this, ignite a candle, and allow it to run for several minutes. Then, you can extinguish the candle, and then put an oil drop in the wax that has been melted, then ignite the candle. Take care, because essential oils are extremely flammable! The goal is to keep the oil within the wax, and not next to the flames in order to prevent it from exploding.

Reed diffusion

It is an extremely known diffusion method. The method is based on the idea that an reed will be placed into an ointment containing dilute essential oils. The reed absorbs oil, and the oil is pushed upwards by the reed. The fluid moves as it shifts it is able to diffuse the oil particles within the air.

Fan diffusion.

It could also be helpful. For this method, an air diffuser uses fans to push essential oils into the air. The fan is blown through an empty tray or pad to be placed in the overall system. The air blowing from the fan travels through the tray and raises the levels of the oil particles that are within the air.

Other options

There are many other types of diffusers available in the market. They vary in terms of the size, quality as well as the strength of the fragrance that is released throughout the space. Certain are more suited and suitable for your own, while others can manage a room. Certain types of diffusers are likely to produce greater focus than others. this is why it's recommended to study the diverse types of diffusers in order to come to your own mind about which will best suit your needs.

Chapter 23: Storing Essential Oils

The most important thing to bear at heart about the essential oils is they will not go through the process of deterioration. This is why storing essential oils can be quite simple by taking a few precautions to ensure safety. These are typically offered in small bottles. If you're making your own mixes there are a variety of size bottles (bear be aware that, if the mix contains the perishable oil that will limit your ability to preserve the mix).

Essential oils are not likely to perish, they can become less useful and degrade. Certain oils may even undergo oxidation and shed their fragrance as well as therapeutic benefits. But, that isn't an issue for any oils. It is suggested to keep your oils in a transparent (yet non-transparent) bottle.

Amber or blue bottles are the most efficient in this regard due to the fact that they're likely to block the sunlight that will try to penetrate the essential oils. Dark glass is the ideal choice to store all your essential oils, but especially the ones that may cause phototoxicity because they're more susceptible to adverse effects of sunlight.

In reality, it's as a matter that you should use dark glass, and you should avoid buying oils that are sold in transparent containers. It is not possible to be able to establish how long this oil was stored in a transparent container. Furthermore, it could be exposed to light, and then decreased its efficiency. Watch out for bottles that use stoppers made of rubber too. Though it may seem to be a great idea but a stopper made of rubber could be gummy because of the oil's high concentration and should be kept away from the bottle. The oil that is kept in a bottle helps guarantee that you don't have an oil leakage.

A thing to keep in the mind is that bottles made of aluminum can be used to store items in the event that they're lined interior. Anything that isn't lined is not suitable for use.

Keep the essential oils you require in a cold, dark place they're not exposed to sunlight and maintained at a moderately low temperature. This is the best way to ensure they're likely to last for longer than is possible. It is very likely that heat will accelerate the process of deterioration, as is sunlight, which could cause your oil to deteriorate.

Chapter 24: Aromatherapy And How It Can Help You

Aromatherapy is the practice of using essential oils, as well as various plant-based ingredients to bring balance to our body, mind and soul. This is a natural method of treatment unlike the chemical substances and the invasive methods that are commonly used in Western medical practices. Although there are those who claim aromatherapists sell only snake oil, there's an increasing number of people who have tried essential oils the strength of they truly are.

Aromatherapy can be used to improve the physical as well as emotional wellbeing and health. It's not an untruth to assert that essential oils are used to heal all illnesses but it's not far to claim that they can be used with occasionally, as a substitute for Western medical treatments to treat various physical and emotional problems.

Essential oils also referred to as ethereal, volatile oils, are derived from organic material of plants. They're the concentrated aroma from the plant they've taken from. The essential oils of plants give the distinctive scent. Alongside the scent, essential oils are a source of various naturally-occurring substances known as being beneficial for the body. They're loaded with nutrients minerals, vitamins, and a variety of useful chemicals that can help your body in numerous ways. They're 100% natural and your body recognizes them in the same way.

For a better understanding of the motivation of aromatherapy, all you need to do is take the word down. "Aroma" means fragrance and "therapy" means treatment. Aromatherapy is a fundamental approach to alleviate a myriad of ailments using essential oils from plants that help to balance the body. It leaves you feeling refreshed and healthy.

The inhalation of scents from essential oils is among the most important applications of aromatherapy. Alongside the inhalation of essential oils, they can also be applied to the skin and oils are even ingested in smaller quantities. Based on the way of application, oils interact with your body's tissues by interacting with your body in the following ways:

They are able to rebalance and alter the internal chemistry through adding positive chemicals, and eliminating toxic substances.

They move through the body to aid in internal processes.

They directly affect the subject in which they're applied.

They can improve your mental wellbeing and mood.

The real power of aromatherapy is in the fact that it works on all the above aspects at the same time. The result is that you are healthier, feel healthier and increase your overall health.

Western medicine, on contrary, is comprised of aggressive medications and treatments to treat diseases and diseases. Even though these therapies might be required to address more serious health problems that cannot be treated with aromatherapy, smaller health problems tend to be better addressed with natural remedies. It's not uncommon for a person who is healthy to take a prescribed medication and experience an allergic reaction. The physician does what he's experienced to do, and then prescribes additional medicine to treat any adverse effects from the initial medication. If more issues arise the doctor prescribes more medicines. In the shortest time, a person becomes too unbalanced chemically that larger troubles begin to manifest themselves, problems which might not have revealed their ugly faces were it not for the fact that the patient was pounding their body repeatedly with the pounding of synthetic drugs.

I witnessed this happen in the first person through my father. He was injured in his back while during work, and was given an extremely light dose of codeine for his back pain. Codeine was a cause of nausea, and high blood pressure and, instead of stopping my father from taking the medication the doctor recommended more drugs to address new issues. The insomnia set in, and then sleeping medications were prescribed as well as valium to aid to rest. Soon, the person I'd never witnessed consume a drug throughout his entire life began taking many more tablets that Charlie Sheen on a bender. The strain was for his body, and harder on his family to witness him suffer through the process. When we attempted to speak with him about the issue but he just seemed to declare that it was okay due to the fact that his doctor had prescribed the medication. The pills he took were consumed until the end of his life, and then his body began to collapse from the burden that he'd placed on it for years.

Overmedicating is a common places across the globe. There's a good chance you won't meet one person who doesn't most know somebody who's taken medication up to the point of uncoherence by medical professionals who practice modern medicine.

Many of the issues that physicians typically prescribe medications for are often treated with aromatherapy. Although I wouldn't recommend stopping using modern medicines completely for treating serious illness and conditions, I advise discussing the benefits of natural remedies with your physician and an aromatherapy expert. You might be surprised to learn that you can utilize aromatherapy alongside or instead of contemporary treatments. It's a fact that in the proper hand, essential oils are an effective tool that could be employed for a vast variety of health reasons.

Here are a few of the numerous therapeutic properties essential oils have

Antibacterial.

Antifungal.

Anti-inflammatory.

Antimicrobial.

Antioxidant.

Antiparasitic.

Antiseptic.

Antispasmodic.

Antiviral.

Boosts immune system.

Calming.

Decongestant.

Increased circulation.

Improved digestion.

Healthier mental state.

Improvement in organ function.

The skin is moisturized.

Relief from pain.

Relaxing.

Skin care.

Skin healing.

Stimulating.

Helps fight cancer.

Well-being.

One of the best things about essential oils is the fact that even a single oil could provide several of these benefits and can be combined with other essential oils to make interesting blends that are delicious and provide an even greater variety of advantages for health. There are hundreds of essential oils available on the market, with the possibility of making several hundred thousand mixtures that have different characteristics. The options are limitless.

A Brief History of Aromatherapy

Although the words "aromatherapy" and "essential oil" are fairly modern, the usage of plants oils for improving health has existed in one form or in another form for thousands of years.

The earliest evidence of oils from plants dates to a time of about 6,000-7,000 B.C. When our early ancestors realized that they could mix the vegetable oils and animal fats and utilize the mixture to cure ailments, heal wounds, as well as relax minds after a long day of gathering and hunting. Although most films of the present depict cavemen as smelly Neanderthals it is possible that they be pretty smelly due to the oils of plants they mixed with fats and rubbing the body.

When man's evolution took place, so did the types of oils utilized and methods employed to get the oils. Instead of mixing organic matter into the animal fat, and then making it cook until the oil was extracted the distillation process and press methods have been discovered which allowed the extraction of huge quantities of concentrated oils that had intense scents as well as therapeutic effects. The oils were extremely sought-after and it was common to see ships travel around the world to have access to precious oils such as sandalwood, frankincense and myrrh. and patchouli.

Ships from all kinds of sizes travelled through the seas high to gain access to oil that was not readily available in the home market and trade deals worth millions today in dollars were concluded between different nations. We don't know for certain the fact that oils essential to life were among the first items traded at a massive scale between nations. However, certain of the first recorded trades included large quantities of myrrhh, cypress and various other oils.

Since the logistical challenges of travelling via land proved too daunting to manage, international trade routes that ran for hundreds of years were developed. Egyptians, Romans and Europeans were all on these routes in order to access the oil available throughout The Middle East, the Orient as well as Africa. Much of the explorations of the globe were accomplished by explorers such as Marco Polo and Christopher Columbus who travelled the world seeking smaller routes that would lead to far-off regions where they could make trade with exotic oils and spices.

Essential oils quickly spread throughout all over the world. They were used by everybody from queens and monarchs as well as the poor and working class. Essential oils were soon adopted by religions due to their religious qualities and further establishing them in the popular society. The usage of essential oils to perform religious ceremonies is embedded in almost every religion around the world. If they're not using essential oils, then they have at some time. The Bible lists a few essential oils in the form of names. Essential oils like frankincense as well as myrrh have been well-known since the present day due to the fact that they were given to Christ by wise men who were able to visit Jesus from a distance. They are also mentioned in the Bible that leads a lot people who consider themselves faith-based to be of the opinion that God has provided essential oils to us for usage.

Essential oils formed the primary and the most important connection between East as well as the West As it transpired the exchange of more than just scents were traded. Technologies advanced both sides because different cultures adopted the inventions and ideas introduced from foreign traders.

Aromatherapy was born from the melting of animal fats as well as plants for the creation of crude aromatherapy precursors of contemporary massage oils. The plants and herbs were frequently used to clean and impart scent in the air. The result was the invention of incense made through the mixing of plant matter with things that made it in the form of a gel and then harden. Incense was soon incredibly popular due to its ease of utilize and to transport. When it was spread around the world It was utilized for anything from purifying the air and warding off bad spirits. In the past, it was not just burned as it is nowadays. It was applied to the skin, eaten in a diet staple, in baths as well as saunas.

The popularity of incense grew as did the usage of oils from plants. The Egyptians made oils that were so potent that the kings' tombs are filled with pots which still bear evidence of the fragrance oils used to store. They became integral components in fragrances and used to help people smell and feel great simultaneously. Massage oils gained popularity as people combined and matched various oils, and then rubbed them on the muscles of their bodies to ease discomfort and ease tension. The oils were used to assist to ease headaches, digestion issues and anxiety. Through the years many thousands of applications for essential oils have been found that cover all kinds of skin problems, from dry and inability to get out of sleep. Although the scientific basis behind these oils was not fully understood until recent times, the fact that people were aware was the fact that they could combat a variety of ailments and diseases. Over the centuries essential oils have been used as a primary treatment option for a variety of people across the world.

It wasn't until around the turn of the century that the oil-based essential oils were beginning to become distinct from medicines. A rise in the the popularity of chemical perfumes that had no benefits for health was the main reason for this separation in the beginning, when people started to see fragrances as things that smell good but with no benefit to health. Modern drugs gained popularity quickly with the introduction of synthetic chemicals on the market, claiming to cure every ailment. Even though many of the initial treatments didn't prove as effective but they did push holistic medicine into the realm of non-existence when the world of civilisation was reliant on Western remedies to treat the ailments of their people.

In the later 1920's when a man called Rene-Maurice Gattfosse "discovered" the healing benefits of essential oils. He injured his hand

and then dipped the hand in lavender essential oil to alleviate the painfulness. A quick healing time after the accident led to discovery essential oils as a therapy remedy. Gattefosse invented the term aromatherapy as well as write a variety of books on the advantages from essential oils. Motivated by his research (and those of many others who joined in the quest) the plant oils gradually but surely found return to the spotlight, but not at the level of fame they had previously enjoyed.

Over the past decade or around the essential oils industry has experienced an increase in popularity as people search at alternatives to Western medical. The modern practitioners of aromatherapy utilize essential oils to enhance the overall health of their patients in a natural way. People who are aware are rapidly recognizing that how modern medicine isn't as it appears to be.

Chapter 25: How Essential Oils Are Used

Essential oils get into your body via the following methods: via the lungs and nose by the skin or via your digestive tract. Inhale their scent, eat the oil, or apply it to the skin for maximum benefits. For you to reap the maximum benefits of your essential oils it is essential to know how in delivering the oils to your body in a way that does not alter the chemical makeup of the oil, and can provide you with the greatest benefits to your health from the essential oils. There many ways for this.

Before getting into all the different ways you can make use of essential oils, I'd like to be clear about one thing. Certain oils don't be suited to certain uses. Certain oils are too harsh for inhalation, certain oils are hot enough to be "hot" to be applied on the body as well, and then there's several oils that should not ever, and I do mean not be consumed. It is important to study the oils you're thinking of applying to determine what is the ideal application for these specific oils.

A mistake could degrade your health, instead of improving it.

Essential oils are best utilized in tiny amounts. When you add a new oil to your collection of tricks, you should make sure to dilute the oil thoroughly and test it on an unnoticed area prior to using the oil on a bigger space. There's a better chance of finding you're allergic or sensitive to an oil after you've just used just a tiny amount rather than slathering massaging oil on the body, and suffering from an all-encompassing negative reaction.

To aid in aromatherapy essential oils are not to be taken orally. The consumption of essential oils is not the most effective way for delivering them as they must pass through your digestive system before making their journey to the body. The powerful acids that are present in your stomach could cause damage to the chemical components in the oil and diminish or even eliminate the benefits you'd get if the oil been applied different ways. There are certain situations where ingestion of oil can be more beneficial than spreading it on top or dispersing the oil, however those instances are very few and rare. One example is oil taken ingestion for digestion purposes or stomach pain. Don't take any oil or blend of oils without consulting your physician. Inhaling essential oils isn't a part of aromatherapy.

Topical Application

If you apply a topically applied essential oil, you are delivering the oil to your body through application directly onto the skin. The process is generally achieved by diluting the oil using the carrier oil however there may be times where oils that are weaker can be used with full force. We'll to look at some different methods you can apply essential oils on the body.

Direct Application (Neat)

This is the most risky type of topically applied application since it involves applying essential oils directly onto the skin the maximum power. The direct application of the oil is described as clean application in certain publications.

A sloppy application is not recommended in all cases, not just the weakest of oils. If you experience an allergic reaction that causes sensitization of your skin, you might discover that your body is unable to tolerate the oil each time you come to contact after it, no matter the amount of dilute you use prior to applying it. Itching, skin rashes burning, and a variety of other ailments can happen as your body's reaction is negative after a well-applied essential oils.

There are a lot of risks Always consult your doctor or an aromatherapy professional before applying the oil in a neat. There are many sites and publications that provide the oils that they claim can be used neat, yet do not have the safety of. Yes, many people might never experience a reaction but if you're a member of those who experience a reaction then you could pay for a price that is high.

There are a number of websites advertising a neat application dubbed the Raindrop method. This is based on dripping several drops of various oils along and down the spine, and let them soak into. It's a risky technique of application since you'll end up putting an amount of the oil on your skin without diluting it. It increases your risk of experiencing a reaction.

Massage Oil

Essential oils may be dilute in carrier oil before being applied to the skin. Carrier oils are those composed of animal or vegetable fat that's not as powerful like essential oils. They don't possess the same power that essential oils have, however they're usually considered beneficial oils that could be used to improve essential oils, and to dilute their effects to the point where they're safe to apply on the skin.

The amount that you need to mix the carrier oils with essential oils is contingent on the quality of the oils that you're applying, but a good standard is to blend 3 and 6 drops of essential oils into one teaspoon of carrier oil. Make sure to keep it at the lower portion at first, until you've tested your skin to determine whether it's sensitive to the oils that you're using. If you intend to apply the cream to areas that are sensitive like your face, reduce it further. You can start with one or two drops of oil, then test it to determine what happens. There is always the option of adding an additional drop in the future if you do not achieve the desired result.

Direct Application (Diluted)

Dilute your essential oils with carrier oil before applying directly on the skin, without massaging it within. Choose a place and lightly massage the oil blend onto the skin. It will absorb fairly quickly, and then leave a protective layer over the skin. Many people dislike this layer and complain that they feel their skin is heavy or greasy. Others love it due to the fact that they feel the coating protects their skin from harmful elements.

Bath Time

Essential oils are a great addition to bath water for the perfect warm and relaxing bathing experience that leaves your body and mind refreshed, as well as the skin and body looking refreshed. It is possible to use aromatic oils during the day to help to get ready for your morning. Change to sedatives or relaxing oils later in the evening, to relax before going to going to bed.

To get the best results To get the most benefit, add 5 to 10 drop total of oils in the water in your bath while taking a bath. Reduce the more harsh oils down to less than 3 drops, and mix oils that have similar properties. A good example is to add just a couple of drops from lavender as well as Roman Chamomile into your bath to end the day, to ease your mind and relax.

Additionally, you can include a couple of drops of your preferred oil to a footbath, and allow your feet to soak in the bath for some time. Do not apply more than 4 or five drops of oil into the foot bath. Use relaxing oils and stay clear of products that could cause irritation to the skin.

Compress

Your sink is filled to capacity with water that is cold or hot. It should be hot as well as as cold as you are able to bear the temperature. Include a couple of drops of essential oil to the water, and mix it. The oil should get to the top of the water, then use an unfolded towel to absorb the oil. Massage the compress onto muscles that are sore or to the body part which you would like to get the most from the compression. Do not apply the compress to areas of your body that are sensitive such as the neck or face, and make sure you don't let any oils-infused water in the eyes. The compress can be left on for 45 to 60 minutes.

If you experience irritation take the compress off and clean off any oil that has accumulated.

Create Your Own Product

It takes more work than other methods and isn't as easy, however it's enjoyable to develop skincare products and lotions specifically designed for your skin's needs and type. Start with a base lotion or lotion, and then include a couple of drops of your preferred essential oils to the mixture. It is possible to make products for your skin, face and body or lotions, as well as salves and a myriad of other goods after you have a better understanding of what different essential oils can be used for.

Inhalation

The inhalation of the aromas of essential oils is an effective method to bring the beneficial health effects of essential oils to the body. Inhaling essential oils, molecules are introduced directly into the bloodstream and quickly spread across the body. As well as being absorbed into the bloodstream, they also interact with the brain after they enter the olfactory receptors within your nasal cavity.

There are many ways to take in the scents. The hot methods, which involve heating the oil to diffuse them in rooms, are usually thought to be less efficient as cold ones since heating the oils could alter their chemical composition. In this section, we'll examine both cold and hot methods here.

Direct Inhalation

Direct inhalation occurs by inhaling the pure aroma of essential oils. These methods of direct inhalation are widely used

A few drops of oil onto an old napkin or a handkerchief, and place it on your nose. Take a deep breath.

Use a tiny amount of the oil in a diluted form onto the top of your lips. Inhale deeply.

Apply a couple of drops of an oil that is weaker in between the palms of your hands. Make a cup with your hands, and put them on your mouth and nose. Take a deep breath and breathe in the aroma.

Remove the cap from the bottle with the oil. Bring it up to just a few inches from your nostrils and inhale the fragrance.

Then fill your sink with hot water. Add 5-10 drops of oil to the water. Put a towel on your head. Hold your head over the sink, and breathe in the steam.

Diffusion

Essential oils can be diffused throughout rooms to provide a more lasting impact. Diffusers evaporate the oil and scatter tiny molecules of oil around the area. They are used for purifying the air as well as to treat ailments. It is a great benefit that everyone present in the space can take advantage of the benefits as well as pleasant aromas.

There are numerous varieties of diffusers that are available in the marketplace. Some utilize heat, but was previously discussed as being unsuitable for the essential oil diffusion. Some prefer cool air, that is the most popular way to distribute essential oils whenever it's feasible. Below are a few modern methods to diffuse essential oils:

Candle diffusers.

Diffusers that warm wax cubes. These are similar to Scentsy warmers.

Dispersers that make use of the light bulb.

Electric diffusers with an element of heating.

Incense filled with oil that's then ignited to release scent.

Although it's well-known that this method isn't ideal however, they're used. A lot of people aren't aware that heating can have a negative impact on essential oils. Many people know this, yet aren't too concerned about the health benefits associated with essential oils or are merely employing them to make the space they're diffusing them to smell nice.

The cold diffusion method is generally believed to be more effective as they do not heat the oil prior to dispersing the aroma into the air. There are a variety of methods to distribute oil without heating it

A small cotton ball, soaked in oil, and then put in a bowl, can efficiently disperse scent throughout the space.

Atomizers and nebulizers convert oils into fine mist, which then diffuses across the room. If you decide to use this technique make sure you only do only for a short period for a period of time. The large amounts of oil get rapidly dispersed and you do not want to be wasting oil or cause irritation to the mucous membranes of your mouth. This approach is great for large spaces and also in circumstances where you need greater amounts of oil dispersed throughout the air.

Fans diffusers blast cool air over the reservoir that contains essential oils combined with water. The aroma is released to the surrounding area.

Reed diffusers utilize pots of oil in the which long sticks of wood are set. The oil moves through the sticks, and the fragrance is diffused throughout the space.

Terra clay pots are filled with oil, the lid is then placed onto the lid. The oil slowly saturates the pores of the clay and spreads throughout the space.

There is the option of adding up to 10 drops essential oils into a spray bottle of water. You can use it to disperse a fine mist oil in a room.

Injecting large amounts of essential oils into the air or spraying it directly onto painted surfaces could harm paint and cause it to appear cracked and peel. Make sure to use the oil in a controlled manner and do not spray it directly on the surface of a painting.

Olfactory Fatigue

You've been to a place where the smell was particularly pleasant or bad, and realized it was a short time later that you became accustomed to the smell and didn't be able to smell it? The reason is that your body began to get used to the scent in a process called Olfactory fatigue took over.

To comprehend the olfactory fatigue phenomenon, it is necessary look back in time to the earliest times to examine the functions that scent was employed for back at the time. In the past, smell was used to detect two essential things that were important: food and risk. Man of the primitive age needed to sense something immediately and know whether it was an omen food item, something worth eating or something that should be avoided. The other smells were a distraction. In the event that a scent which did not resemble food nor was it dangerous made its route to the brain, the brain processed it before dismissed it as not important so that it can focus on other scents that enter the brain which could be more relevant.

Olfactory fatigue can be described as the modern contemporary variation of the threat food analysis. If you notice something smelly over a long duration of time but do not give it the priority you deserve the brain thinks the smell is not important, and then discards the scent. It becomes immune to the smell for as long as you stay in the same area. It's the reason workers can to be in sewers that smell over long durations and also farmers reside on farms with massive amounts of manure. The smell of manure is evident while you drive around the neighborhood, but the workers and farmers are there for all day long and don't have the stench anymore.

Then, leaving the space surrounded by the smell and then taking the scent away out of the area and then re-releasing it allows that you can smell the scent again in a limited amount duration because your brain needs to process the scent again. When your brain process the scent, it will be able to dismiss this scent as insignificant and at a faster rate each time it presents it. After a while, your body is almost immune to the smell. The brain is aware of it and process it instantly.

This is why essential oils are best used in small amounts and for short durations. Five to 10 minutes of short bursts of fragrance are effective than saturating rooms with scent for hours. If you're in a space when you discover that you cannot notice a scent anymore Don't assume that there's no scent in the diffuser. You can make sure to add. You may have been unable to smell the fragrance because of olfactory fatigue. You can leave the room for one-half hour, then come back. You may be shocked by the smell of it again, at the very least, for a brief amount of time.

Setting your electronic diffusers to an alarm will give you to have a certain amount of control over the frequency at which oil diffuses throughout a space. This is a great option with light oils which have high notes, but don't hang in the air for long. Certain essential oils are bulky and are known to hang throughout a room for several long periods of time or for days following the dispersal. What should you do? Simple. Spread the oil around an area that you do not devote a lot of hours in. You can then go to the room for 20-30 minutes when you believe you require some of the advantages that the oil can provide. Alter the oils you're using every now and then so that your brain is constantly occupied.

Measuring Essential Oils

There are many measurement methods for essential oils, it could turn your head. Ounces, milliliters, drops, etc. There's no universal measure that can be used for all purposes. This chapter has been intended to take away the confusion of weighing the quality of your oil.

The most popular way to measure in recipes using essential oils, is the drop. One of the problems when using drops for measuring oil is that it may mean different things for one person than it would to another. A person may think the drop is from an eyedropper, whereas someone else might think that a drop is from the turkey baster. This could result in two persons getting totally differing (and possible risky) outcomes from their respective oils. We'll get it straight right now. One Drop of essential oil can be considered to be an average drop taken from an eyedropper. There could be slight variations in size between drops, but it is not enough to be of concern in the making of any of the largest quantities of oil blends and items.

There isn't a standard weight of a drop since essential oils come with various densities, and they weigh in different quantities. The range of drops can vary from 20-plus 50 drops of oil. You could be spending hours studying the oil quantities but it's not necessary. We can suppose that 20 drops of oil equals one mL. You can you can go to the next level. There's always the option of adding more essential oils to your recipes in the future when the results don't match what you were hoping for.

Although drops can be a good way to measure small quantities of oil blends or products but you'll need an easier way of measuring for taking larger quantities of oil. No one wants to sit and count 1000 drops oil for a huge batch. Milliliters or teaspoons, ounces and milliliters all become relevant. You can choose to decide which measurement method you choose to use. All three methods will be covered in this chapter since there are plenty of recipes using any one of these three methods.

The following chart is one you'll need to carry around with you:

Unit of Measurement	Converts to
20 drops	1 milliliter (mL)
100 drops	1 tablespoon (tsp)
300 drops	1 teaspoon (tbsp)
600 drops	1 one ounce (oz)
1 tablespoon (tsp)	5 milliliters (mL)

1 tablespoon (tsp)   1/6 one ounce (oz)

Three teaspoons (tsp)   1 teaspoon (tbsp)

Three teaspoons (tsp)   1 an ounce (oz)

6. teaspoons (tsp)   1 Ounce (oz)

1 teaspoon (tbsp)   15 milliliters (mL)

1 teaspoon (tbsp)   1 one ounce (oz)

2 Tablespoons (tbsp.)   1 Ounce (oz)

1 ounce (oz)   15 milliliters (mL)

1 Ounce (oz) 30 milliliters (mL)

Remember that these calculations can be rounded off or calculated to facilitate ease to usage. It is possible to calculate precise amounts if you wish however it's not important and the majority of people follow these measurements in mixing small quantities of oil. The greater the quantity of oil you mix is the more likely it will be important whether you make use of precise measurement. If you're one of the people who makes essential oils in their homes for personal use The chart provided is sufficient.

When you're mixing larger quantities it is necessary to weigh your oils or gauge them by volume in order to ensure that the blends are accurate. Anything over a few inches should be accurately measured to make sure there's the proper quantity of oils in the blends. If you're going to weigh your oils, invest in the best weighing scale which is exact to one tenth of the Gram. If you're planning to measure via volume, get the best pipettes and beakers which are clearly marked within the scale you intend to use.

If you're mixing oils, it is possible to come across recipes requiring proportions, not real units of measurement. When an oil or oil blend demands the dilution to be 5%, you must figure out how much 5% of amount of carrier oil that you are planning to utilize in addition to that essential oils. If you're using just 1 tablespoon of carrier oil the 5% reduction would equal approximately five drops of essential oils. If you own one instance of carrier oil that weighs an ounce, the 5% concentration could be equivalent to .05 for an ounce essential oil, or 30 drops.

How to calculate the amount of essential oil required is:

The quantity of carrier oil percent of diluting

Change the percentage into decimal before adding. 55% becomes .05.

This chart will help you understand some calculations for you. to help you get started:

Amount of Carrier Oil	Dilution Percentage	Amount of Essential Oil to Use
1 tablespoon (tsp)	10%	10 drops
1 teaspoon (tbsp.)	10%	30 drops
1 one ounce (oz)	10%	60 drops
1 tablespoon (tsp)	5%	5 drops

www.ingramcontent.com/pod-product-compliance
Lightning Source LLC
Chambersburg PA
CBHW062138020426
42335CB00013B/1253